THE
BATTLE-READY
BELIEVER

BY MICHAEL BOLDEA, JR.

OTHER BOOKS BY MICHAEL BOLDEA, JR.

The Holy Spirit: Power, Presence, and Purpose

Fundamental Doctrines: Understanding the Elementary Principles of Christ

When Ye Pray: The Anatomy of Prayer - Book One (Volume 1)

When Ye Pray: Prayers of the Old Testament - Book Two (Volume 2)

365 Thoughts, Meditations & Words of Wisdom: A Daily Devotional

WATERTOWN, WISCONSIN

BOLDMAN PUBLISHING
WATERTOWN, WISCONSIN

www.handofhelp.com

THE BATTLE-READY BELIEVER

ISBN-13:978-1537519135

ISBN-10:1537519131

All Scripture taken from the New King James edition.

TABLE OF CONTENTS

ACKNOWLEDGMENTS

For Amy, April, and Susan without whose tireless help
much of what I write would still be relegated
to the hard drive of my computer.

Thank You!

INTRODUCTION

We are living amidst a generation of spiritual marshmallows. A disproportionate number of those calling themselves soldiers for Christ and warriors of the cross know nothing of spiritual warfare, the weapons employed in said warfare, or what it means to stand one's ground before the onslaught of the enemy. By and large they are soft, sickly sweet with political correctness, full of air, and melt at the first sign of heat just like a marshmallow.

We have replaced character and moral fortitude with insolent condescension, and rather than aspire to spiritual greatness like those who came before us, we find reasons to demean them and degrade their accomplishments on behalf of the Kingdom.

Since when do the latest fashionable trendsetters with questionable degrees from online seminaries, have the right to question Paul, Peter, John, Luke, Mark, or even Jesus Himself?

Since when does a spiritual homunculus have the right to contradict the Word of God itself, and still have the temerity to call himself a pastor of one of the largest congregations in the world?

In the estimation of this present generation, martyrs were only martyrs because they weren't bright enough to doubletalk their way out of their predicaments. There is little to no understanding of duty in today's modern church, and what passes for spiritual maturity is a cross between pathetic and terrifying.

When compromise becomes our banner and cowardice is seen as virtue, is it any wonder that so few among professing believers today are battle-ready?

We have been seduced. We have become so enamored with the world and this present life that we give no thought to the reality that eternity beckons with every breath, and that the enemy's sole purpose is to keep us from spending eternity with God.

A battle is coming whether the church is ready for it or not. The enemy has assembled his armies, they have amassed on the battlefield, and in short order the final assault against the children of God will commence.

The level of your spiritual readiness will determine whether you will survive the battle or be so much fodder having fallen like so many others. One cannot prepare for battle on the battlefield. One cannot begin to know the weapons of his warfare as the enemy is charging and the air is thick with the expectation of battle.

In understanding that battle is inevitable the wise will ready themselves in advance, learning what it is to be a soldier and taking the necessary steps to become it.

Men wage war for various reasons at various times. While some are compelled by patriotism or religious beliefs, others are driven by ambition or lust for power. Whatever the underlying reason for war, it is powerful enough to cause an individual to risk their life for it.

In any battle, in any war, the possible loss of one's life is implied. There has never been a war waged without casualties, and every individual who enlists does so with the full knowledge that it may very well mean their life.

Physical war is bloody, brutal, and taxing in every way possible. What believers seem to have forgotten over the years is that spiritual warfare is just as brutal, just as taxing, and just as ruthless as any war in the physical. Spiritual warfare also carries greater far-reaching consequences than war in the natural does, because the consequences of spiritual warfare are eternal in their scope.

Wherever I happen to be on any given Sunday it seems I hear more about the victory party after the battle than I do about the battle itself anymore. Preachers don't like to preach on spiritual warfare. Parishioners don't like to hear about spiritual warfare, and so we focus on the hereafter instead. We focus on that moment beyond time when the last sword will have been swung and the last blow will have been struck, utterly failing to prepare or even make the individual aware of the war they are currently embroiled in.

If you call yourself a son or daughter of God, then you are at war. Since the fact that you are already at war is a foregone reality and you have no say in the matter, would it not be wise and prudent to learn all you can about your enemy and about the weapons you have at your disposal?

Would it not be wisdom itself to learn how we can defend ourselves and even go on the offensive against an enemy who has already made it perfectly clear that he will take no prisoners?

Even though the spectator stands are overflowing and the warriors on the field of battle are decreasing in number at an alarming rate, we who remain cannot give up the fight. We cannot lay down our arms, we cannot take off our armor, and we cannot surrender to the enemy, for if we do we will be counted among the rebellious and disobedient. We will be counted among those who ought to have known what it is to stand, to fight, and to overcome an enemy who fears our General, and who has given us the privilege and right to walk in His authority.

Many claim bravery when there is no call for it, but very few exhibit bravery in the face of certain violence or mortal danger. In modern day parlance many Christians talk a good game, but when their mettle is tested, when the battle is upon them, they turn tail and run. They surrender to the enemy, or worse still become traitors to the cause of Christ attempting to weaken the household of faith from within.

If all we can do is talk a good game, if we have not trained, equipped, prepared, and honed our spiritual selves, when the day of battle is upon us, though we may think ourselves brave, though we may think ourselves steadfast, we will flee from the onslaught of the enemy.

Battle presupposes many things, but certain ones are essential. Among the essentials of any conflict are armies, arms, tactics, strategy, and the knowledge of one's adversary. If any of these essentials is missing, one's loss of the battle is ensured even before the first blow is struck.

Without having the right soldiers, the right arms, the right strategy and a fundamental understanding of one's enemy, we are inhibited and stunted in our ability to fight the fight in such a manner that victory is certain.

Brutal and coldhearted as it may seem, one need only give a passing glance to the current church to realize that though we might call ourselves an army we are weaponless, absent of strategy, ignorant of tactics, and woefully unaware of our enemy, what he can do, and the lengths he will go to in any conflict.

A soldier's ignorance of his weapons on the battlefield will almost always ensure his demise. If he stands face to face against his enemy and does not know how to wield his sword, raise his shield, or have a passing knowledge of all the weapons in his arsenal, that moment of hesitation, the fumbling with one's scabbard, the overreach of one's sword, the wrong placement of one's shield, and the enemy will strike the mortal blow.

By the same token, a soldier who does not know the tactics of his enemy or how to defend against them is at a serious disadvantage on the battlefield. We are warned, and forthrightly so in God's word, not to be ignorant of the devil's devices. The reason this warning is found within the pages of scripture is because once we are aware of the devil's devices, we will naturally begin to take steps to protect ourselves against them and guard our hearts against their influences.

If battle finds us unprepared, if the enemy finds us defenseless, if we find ourselves standing on the battlefield with no weapons of either defense or offense, know that our ill preparedness was not God's fault but our own. We have been warned and repeatedly so to prepare, to put on our armor, to know how to wield the power granted to us by the blood of the Lamb, and if we have failed to do these things, or believed that they somehow did not pertain to us, we have no one to blame but ourselves.

A wise man prepares. A wise man does his utmost to make certain that he has done his utmost, and then trusts in the arm of God to do what he cannot.

Laziness has made many within the church indifferent toward the reality of the times they are living in and though the Word of God urges us to prepare, to be as faithful soldiers, to know the weapons of our warfare and be diligent about growing spiritually, many roll their eyes and fail at stifling their yawns.

This book is not meant for the indifferent. This book is not meant for the spiritually lazy. This book is meant for those who see the storm clouds on the horizon, those that understand on a very basic level that battle is inevitable, and who realize that they have little time to prepare – but prepare they must.

This book is meant for those searching for truth, those who refuse to buy into the lie that we are impotent in the face of the enemy, that we have no weapons to speak of, or that we are at the mercy of evil and evil men.

We are sons and daughters of the Most High God. We were commanded to stand, and do all to stand, being fearless in our battle against the darkness, knowing that God stands with us, and fights alongside us.

By the end of this book you will hopefully be able to answer the following questions for yourself:

1. Who taught you how to fight?
2. What are you fighting for?
3. How far are you willing to go?
4. Are you mature enough?
5. Have you built up your endurance?
6. Do you understand your authority?
7. Do you know your weapons?
8. Do you know your General?
9. Do you know yourself?
10. Do you know your enemy?
11. Do you know your objective?

These are all questions we must answer individually, being honest with ourselves, and making the requisite changes if and where they are needed.

The time for sailing through our spiritual existence without consequence is far past. The time for spiritual immaturity has long since expired, and though many a man continue to espouse the fallacy that being battle-ready is a choice rather than a requirement, what we are witnessing with our own eyes throughout the world is exposing such men for the liars they are.

In His grace, God has given us time to prepare for the battle. Whether or not we take advantage of this grace and actually do prepare spiritually is a matter placed wholly and solely on us. God will not do for us what we can do for ourselves nor will He force us to train and exercise our spiritual selves even if we don't want to.

It is incumbent upon us as individuals to understand the days in which we are living and act accordingly. It is incumbent upon us as individuals to put away the childish things, and grow into the warriors God expects us to be.

CHAPTER ONE

WHO TAUGHT YOU TO FIGHT?

In the physical, when it comes to the craft of war and the doing of battle, some men are self-taught, others have teachers, while others enlist in the armed forces where they learn the basics of battle – how to defend themselves, how to fell their enemies – all in a matter of weeks.

For some learning how to fight is a necessity, for others it is a hobby, and for a select few it is an identity, something their entire existence revolves around.

There are warriors and there are warriors. There are men who enlist, put in their time, get their college paid for, and nevermore dwell on combat. Then there are those whose lifelong pursuit is the art of war, and their skillset grows exponentially throughout their lives.

Some men see soldiering as a means to an end, while others see soldiering and learning the finite details of warfare as the end itself.

As battle-ready believers our learning never stops, nor does our training. It becomes so engrained in us, it becomes such an important part of our lives that we learn to exercise our spiritual gifts and go through a checklist of our spiritual weapons each morning upon waking, without fail.

As is the case with most things, repetition is the key to learning and the mother of all skill. In order to have something to repeat and thereby grow skillful at, however, one must have first been taught, and taught by someone who knew what they were talking about.

Unfortunately, the spiritual mirrors the physical in many instances. As is the case in the physical, wherein many an impostor comes off as something they are not and hoodwinks unsuspecting innocents into believing they are black belts in the Martial Arts, there are countless individuals when it comes to spiritual matters that pretend at being men of substance but are nothing more than profiteers and bandits.

These are men who will often boast of themselves, of their accomplishments, but give very little time and make very little effort to highlight their General, to highlight the Christ, and point the way to Him.

True soldiers know that they are one part of the whole, members of one unit, and as such never attempt to steal the spotlight or draw attention to themselves. True soldiers know what it is to work in unity, as a cohesive body, doing their part in ensuring that everyone makes it home alive and with as few wounds as possible.

Just as is the case in the physical, when one member of a unit drops the ball, when they fail to do their duty, when they don't act quickly enough, decisively enough, or wisely enough, the whole body suffers, and is placed in mortal danger.

One bad apple can, and oftentimes does, spoil the bunch. One false teaching with no opposition, one false doctrine with no refutation, one false teacher with no renunciation, and the truth is slowly undermined, the hearts of men turned, and before you know it you have an entire denomination embracing abomination as though it were virtue itself.

Because false doctrine and false teaching often comes via false teachers, I want to spend some time on this oft avoided topic within the household of faith.

Throughout the Word of God, we are warned about false teachers and commanded not to be weary, to be wise, to contend for the faith, and to stand up for truth no matter how unpopular our stance might be.

> *Jude 1:3, "Beloved, while I was very diligent to write to you concerning our common salvation, I found it necessary to write to you exhorting you to contend earnestly for the faith which was once for all delivered to the saints."*

When we are told to contend, we are in fact told to struggle, and by doing so surmount any difficulty or danger. When we are told to contend earnestly, we are in fact told to contend with zeal, steadfastness, and unwavering commitment.

Speak of these things to some in the church and they'll start screaming *'works'* as though their hair was on fire, but it's not me they must contend with, it is the Word of God. More and more I get the feeling that many within the church are simply too lazy to lift a finger in defense of the Gospel, and rather than admit the truth to themselves they'd rather label everyone else a legalist.

It is our duty to fight, to contend, to do battle every time a heresy arises, every time apostasy arises, every time false teachers emerge, and the truth of God is attacked.

> *Jude 1:4, "For certain men have crept in unnoticed, who long ago were marked out for this condemnation, ungodly men, who turn the grace of our God into licentiousness and deny the only Lord God and our Lord Jesus Christ."*

Unfortunately, it is such men – men who have crept in unnoticed – within the household of faith but who have long been marked for condemnation that are growing in popularity and attempting to teach others what it is to be battle-ready when they themselves have not a clue.

Few things stand in starker contrast than the theory of warfare and the practice thereof. Anyone can spout off theory. Anyone can armchair quarterbook a battle that has already taken place, or point out the failures of soldiers who came before them, men and women who fought valiantly, who stood their ground, and who are no more. Anyone can move their hands about and seem as though they know what they are doing, but the tale is told when the rubber meets the road, and when the clash of swords breaks the silence.

Individuals who pretend to know more than they do are a danger to the household of faith as a whole, and to the children of God as individuals. Many a soul take their words for gospel, mimic their actions, and when the time comes to do battle they are trodden underfoot before they realize it.

So the next time we decide to give one of these men a pass, or give them the benefit of the doubt, or defend what they said because we like their bubbling personality, let's stick to the Word. The Word, just so we're clear, calls them ungodly men, and men who were long ago marked out for condemnation.

What is their primary characteristic? Well, turning the grace of God into licentiousness is a good indicator, as is denying the singularity of Jesus, the Divinity of Jesus, the Lordship of Jesus, and the Kingship of Jesus.

Since this is not a book on false teachers, I'll let you figure out who they are on your own!

It is only when we minimize what our enemy's ultimate intent is and how single minded he is about attaining his objective that we become indifferent and even flippant about his minions and what they are doing within the household of faith.

The devil isn't out to bruise you, or skin your knee, or call you nasty names. The devil is out to kill you. What's more, every single individual who does his bidding, every single one roaming about already marked for condemnation, has the selfsame objective in mind.

Men teach heresy for the singular purpose of destroying other men spiritually!

In the end that is the root of every false teaching, false doctrine, and false interpretation. The devil knows the battle he is in but sadly much of the church does not. The devil knows the stakes of this battle but sadly the church seems to have forgotten, thinking that somehow if they are trampled underfoot, if they are overcome rather than overcomers, they'll just end up in a less glitzy part of heaven, but heaven nevertheless.

After outlining a pretty grim picture of the end times, speaking of wars, rumors of wars, and how we would be hated by all nations for His name's sake, Jesus went on to speak some heavy, heavy words for every believer who thinks they can wing it or somehow get through what's coming without being fully equipped, fully trained, and fully sold out for Christ.

Matthew 24:13, "But he who endures to the end shall be saved."

Jesus didn't say *"he who tries, attempts, or thinks they can endure to the end,"* Jesus said, *"he who endures to the end!"*

Valiant efforts won't cut it, nor will halfhearted attempts at enduring. If we believe the words of Jesus – and we have no reason to doubt Him – then only he who endures to the end shall be saved!

The whole point of this book is to prepare you spiritually, and open your eyes to the reality that you are more than what you've been told you are by those pretending to be your spiritual betters. The whole point of this book is to make sure you are a battle-ready believer, and it all begins with who taught you to fight.

If the one who taught you to fight was not taught by Christ, if the one who taught you to fight did not have the Word of God as their foundation, then you don't know how to fight at all. True skill is not flashy; it is efficient. True skill is not interested in entertaining onlookers; it is only interesting in felling its enemy, and permanently so.

We can shadow box until we're blue in the face but until we've taken a punch to the nose, felt tears well up in our eyes, and made the conscious decision to counterattack, all we've been doing is pretend fighting.

The devil is not pretend fighting. He is not pulling punches, and he won't give second chances. This is not a training exercise. This is war, and the church better realize this sooner rather than later. We are at war. Ever since the advent of the household of faith, it has been at war.

As such, feelings, emotions, or opinions are irrelevant. The only thing of import, the only thing of relevance, the only thing that matters is if you were taught to fight by God through His Word, or if the individual who taught you was taught of God. Because the topic of this book oftentimes compels me to be less than gentle in my approach, for those who are not yet ready to hear them, my words may seem downright offensive.

If you are offended, so be it! The stakes are too high, and the outcome of this battle too important for me to try and sugarcoat this in any way in an attempt to spare feelings.

If you were taught by a fool, modeled your life after a fool, and followed after a fool, then you are a fool. If you were taught by Christ, modeled your life after Christ, and followed after Christ, then you are like Christ.

We can try to split hairs but why waste the time?

Once we understand the truth of the battle we find ourselves in, once we understand we are facing an enemy who takes no prisoners, then we will realize just how irrelevant our feelings or bruised egos are.

God doesn't coddle soldiers and we're too old to be infants!

The lateness of the hour is evident to one and all, perhaps with the exception of the church, which is still under the misconception that when the Word tells believers to put on the whole armor of God, somehow it doesn't apply to them but to someone else.

Were you taught to fight by a man of God or a wolf in sheep's clothing? Were you taught to fight by a true shepherd or a hireling whose insistence on your sowing seed and paying tithes bordered on the psychotic?

Did you learn how to fight or were you just sheered of your wool like so many sheep, then left to wander about thinking yourself invincible when in fact you were defenseless?

In your heart you already know the answers to these questions. In your heart you know if you followed after a man of God or after an empty suit. You know who taught you to fight or even if fighting ever came up in between the lengthy sermons on the widow of Zarephath and the prodigal son, because let's face it, spiritual warfare is not high on many a preacher's agenda nowadays. You know! Now all that is required is for you to be honest enough with yourself to admit the truth and take the painful but necessary steps to remedy the situation you find yourself in.

One surefire way to keep from being deceived is to go directly to the source and learn from Jesus Himself. Yes, there are still well intentioned servants from whom you can learn, yes there are still messengers whom God sends, but you must be ever vigilant as to whom you allow to speak into your life, and who you allow to feed you spiritually.

No matter how bright their smile or how crisp their suit, a messenger will always be just a messenger; an envoy of the One who sent him. If they are true servants they will walk in the authority of their Master, and as such wield power. They will also possess the knowledge and ability to do battle, being someone you can learn from. Even so, always keep in mind that to elevate a servant to the position of master is to commit sin.

I learned how to fight from my grandfather. He was a rare man. He was a man who loved God above all else, and his love for God knew no limits or delineations. I spent most of my childhood with my grandfather since my father was at work trying to put food on the table, and throughout my adolescence he taught me love for God. Not with words but with actions.

My grandfather never preached at me. He simply lived his life sold out to God, and this resounded with me more effectively than ten thousand sermons. His love for Jesus was obvious in his everyday life, and this love flowed out of him like a stream.

As I grew older he began to teach me deeper truths, but no matter what it was he taught me it was always tethered in the Word, and he insisted that I search it out for myself.

The first and most important thing my grandfather taught me about spiritual warfare is to always be prepared for battle. The devil is not a gentleman. He doesn't fight fair. If the enemy can attack you when you are not paying attention or are distracted, that is exactly when he will attack.

As men and women of God our duty is to be perpetually hypervigilant for one of the enemy's attacks. We cannot allow the enemy to take us by surprise, and the only way to guard against it is to watch and pray and be vigilant at all times. This does not mean we look for demons under every rock and around every tree. What it means is that we are continually tapped into the spiritual realm, and trust our warrior instincts when it comes to imminent attacks.

God used this principle to select warriors for Gideon. Whether or not they possessed this hypervigilance was one of the ways God whittled down Gideon's army from 10,000 men to 300 men. At first there were 22,000 men, a healthy number to be sure, but after being told that if they were afraid they were free to return to their homes, only 10,000 men remained. Of these 10,000 only 300 lapped water by putting their hand to their mouth, while the rest knelt to drink. A kneeling man starts out at a disadvantage. He cannot defend himself as readily as if he was standing, and by kneeling to drink he diminishes his ability to be aware of his surroundings. God told Gideon to keep only those who were hypervigilant, and with a handful of men, the day was won.

I have been traveling pretty much nonstop since early adolescence. I was twelve years old when I began traveling as my grandfather's interpreter, and although I turned 40 recently I'm still on the road. One of the first things I learned to do no matter where I found myself was to be aware of my surroundings. Whether in downtown Chicago, Istanbul, Miami, Sydney, or a small Amish town in Pennsylvania, my head is always on a swivel, and I am always aware of everything going on around me.

To this day I have not been mugged, held up, carjacked, or menaced in any way, even though I've traveled to dangerous places, and walked through dangerous neighborhoods. The reason I've never had a negative experience in these places is because I know how to gauge a situation, I am perpetually aware of my surroundings, and I act immediately upon getting that intangible feeling in the pit of my stomach.

Experience will teach you to anticipate the enemy's attacks because no matter how well he attempts to camouflage his actions, no matter how well he tries to mask his intent there is always that moment when your hair stands on end, and you get that feeling in your gut that something's coming. Trust those feelings, and be ready for when the attack commences.

The second thing my grandfather taught me when it came to spiritual warfare was to stand one's ground. It matters not whether you are outnumbered, it matters not if you are the only one on the battlefield, stand your ground.

The amazing thing is that once we commit to standing our ground, once we are resolute in our stance that nothing and no one will move us from the spot we are defending, everything becomes crystal clear. All the thoughts, all the doubts, all the second guessing, they all disappear, and all that remains is you doing your all to remain steadfast. It is in those moments of total commitment wherein we are not trying to find a way out of the battle but simply to man our post that we will notice we are being helped and aided by He who is always fighting alongside us.

One of the most legendary and feared group of fighting men at any point in human history were the Cheyenne dog soldiers. The reason they were so feared by anyone who took the battlefield against them is because it was known that they would neither retreat nor surrender, but rather fight to the death.

These men wore sashes of tanned skin across their chests, which were then attached to a picket pin that they would hammer into the ground upon the commencement of battle. These soldiers were effectively staked to the ground and could not move, so there was no option but to fight, and do so without reservation.

Even if you are the only one on the battlefield you are still a majority. You are a one-man or one-woman army because God and the hosts of heaven stand with you. It is this knowledge that must embolden us and give us courage. It is this knowledge that must fuel us and drive us to defend the Gospel and the name of our God.

The third thing I learned from my grandfather regarding doing battle with the enemy is to never trust in oneself. No matter how proficient you become, no matter how mature, no matter how knowledgeable, never trust in the arm of the flesh.

History is littered with the corpses of those who forgot this all-important rule. There are countless examples of men and women who started out on the right path, laboring on behalf of the kingdom, trusting in the arm of God to see them through, then suddenly, without warning, they began to think themselves above the need to give all glory and honor to God. They began to think themselves strong in and of themselves, able to vanquish the enemy without any help, only to find themselves face down in the mud, vanquished and humiliated.

We ought to be wise enough to know our own limitations by now. We ought to be wise enough to acknowledge the presence of God in the midst of our battle, and give Him the glory He deserves for having given us the strength and having fought on our behalf.

It is human nature to try and take credit for things we didn't do, and this is not anything new. This goes back to the beginning of creation, and whenever men had the opportunity to take credit for something God did, for many, the temptation was too much to resist.

It is God who goes before us. It is God who aids us in battle. He is our General, He is our commanding officer, and He will always be on the frontlines of any battle.

God does not lead from behind. He does not simply give orders then hope that His soldiers succeed. God is ever present in the battle, always there to lend a hand, and even when all seems lost, when we see ourselves as outnumbered and the outcome of our endeavor all but lost, God steps in and turns it around in an instant.

If the individual who taught you to fight was proficient, if their purpose was to train you to do battle on your own rather than keep you dependent upon them, then you know what it is to put on your armor and step onto the battlefield. Do so with the full assurance that God stands with you as long as you stand with Him.

Depending on who taught you to fight you will also have a predisposition toward a certain discipline. Some will have a predisposition toward exegesis, others will have predisposition toward certain gifts of the Holy Spirit, others still will have a predisposition toward the prophetic, and although they become well versed in every discipline becoming a complete Christian, those preferences and predispositions exist and carry throughout.

Soldiers recognize other soldiers even if they happen to serve in other branches of the armed forces. True soldiers need not advertise, and they need not put on a beret or wear camouflage pants. Soldiers just know other soldiers either by their demeanor, a look in their eye, or some innate sense that you have happened upon a brother in arms.

I am leery of any man who tries to draw attention to the fact that he is a soldier, and this is doubly true of those who go around telling one and all how they are a spiritual warrior the likes of which the world has never seen.

Titles don't impress me; men of God do. Nowadays anyone can claim any title for themselves, but until they've been in the mud, until they've stared down the enemy, until we can compare scars and tell war stories, your title does nothing to endear me to you.

There are four things we must do as wise followers of Christ when it comes to this all important question of who taught us how to fight and those four things are: identify, analyze, resolve, and take the appropriate action.

1. Identify the individual who taught you to fight.

2. Analyze their life, character, conduct, and fruit thereby determining whether or not they were a true follower of Christ.

3. Resolve whether or not you possess fighting knowhow given who taught you to fight.

4. Take the appropriate action whether that action is starting over and learning anew the art of war, or growing in your skill as a warrior, having a true and right foundation in place.

CHAPTER TWO

WHAT ARE YOU FIGHTING FOR?

If a man has nothing in his life he is willing to die for he has nothing worth living for either. If he has nothing worth living for then he has nothing worth fighting for. Many today, are sitting on the sidelines of the battle because they have not as yet identified what it is they are willing to live for, die for, and yes, fight for to their last. We all fight for something at some point but the something we fight for must be so all encompassing that we are willing, if need be, to lay down our very lives in its service.

When that for which we are fighting does not consume us, when the value we place on either the victory or defeat of our battle does not outweigh our effort, we will put forth a halfhearted effort at best, not really giving it our all in the battle.

What motivates you to fight the fight you are fighting? Is your motivation strong enough to carry you through the pain and the heartache? Is your motivation strong enough to carry you through the hardships and the trials? Is your motivation strong enough to carry you beyond this present life?

I want to begin this chapter by quoting a passage out of Nehemiah, because it goes to another aspect or attribute a battle-ready believer must possess, and that is the knowledge of what it is they are fighting for.

Nehemiah 4:14, "And I looked, and arose and said to the nobles, to the leaders, and to the rest of the people, 'Do not be afraid of them. Remember the Lord, great and awesome, and fight for your brethren, your sons, your daughters, your wives, and your houses.'"

It is of utmost importance to know what we are fighting for. Are we fighting for something temporal or something eternal? Are we fighting for something as fleeting as power, positions, or possessions or are we fighting for something with permanence like the Kingdom of God?

Each time you strap on your armor, each time you unsheathe your sword, each time you lift your shield, what is it you are doing these things for?

Each time you pray for someone, each time you share the gospel, each time you intercede, each time you give of yourself and your possessions, what is it you are doing it for? The answer we give must be clear and concise, without ambiguity. The answer we give will determine the wherewithal with which we do battle, and the ferocity with which we fight, and the energy we exert on behalf of our endeavor.

In attempting to embolden his countrymen Nehemiah reminded them that they were fighting for their brethren, for their sons, for their daughters, for their wives, and their houses. There is nothing more personal, more intimate, and more motivating than fighting for those things you hold most dear, those things which are precious to you. There is nothing more energizing than the realization that you are the last line of defense for your family and your loved ones, and that their wellbeing hinges on the success of your endeavor.

I don't think it would have had the same punch if Nehemiah would have told his countrymen they were fighting for their political party. I don't think it would have had the same punch if Nehemiah would have told his countrymen they were fighting for someone else's lands and possessions. Nehemiah made it personal. He made it intimate. He opened the eyes of his countrymen to the reality that if they lost this battle then they lost everything.

What are you fighting for? This is a question you must know the answer to instantly without giving it any thought because it defines not only the battle but also you as a soldier.

Are you fighting to defend your pet doctrine or are you fighting to defend the truth? Are you fighting to defend a denomination or are you fighting to defend the kingdom of heaven? Are you fighting to defend a man or are you fighting to defend the name of Jesus? These are all questions only you can answer.

I don't know about you but I am fighting for the name of Jesus, for eternity, for heaven, for those I love and care for, and for the Kingdom of God. Because I know what I am fighting for I hold nothing back. I do not try to minimize my effort, hedge my bets, or try to avoid the battle. I know what I'm fighting for and it's precious enough to me that I would readily die for it.

When you know what you are fighting for you will nevermore grow weary, disillusioned, or despair. When you know what you are fighting for you will nevermore look for a way out, just for a way through. We know that our battle is not for earthly things or earthly possessions, but for heavenly things and treasures that do not rust or fade away.

Know what you're fighting for! Know why you're fighting the fight you are fighting! And know that the Lord is with you if you are with Him!

1 Timothy 6:12, "Fight the good fight of faith, lay hold on eternal life, to which you were also called and have confessed the good confession in the presence of many witnesses."

So what motivates you? What promise? What reward? What prize motivates you to the point of forfeiting this present life and all its baubles for the reality of battle, day in and day out?

This in the end is what it must come down to. If we are soldiers of the cross, if we are warriors for Christ, if we are the army of God, then the only thing we must know, the only thing we can know is battle.

We've been lied to. Repeatedly, consistently, unashamedly, the household of faith has been lied to! We've been told by grinning fools that all one need do in order to obtain eternal life is be a good person, consider ourselves spiritual, try not to do bad things, don't swear so much anymore, and of course, give ten percent of our money to the selfsame grinning men making these assertions.

As such, the notion of fighting the good fight has been lost from the collective hearts and minds of the church, and whenever the great majority hears of such a thing they are taken aback. Many reject the notion of battle outright, because it would actually mean that they exert themselves, break a sweat, put down the TV clicker, or do something out of their comfort zone.

The church has grown lazy and we love to have it so. There is nothing required of us except for the few bucks we put in the offering basket, or the check we write to our favorite ministry. We love the spiritual leaders who encourage our spiritual slothfulness because they get us. We fawn over them and elevate them to godlike status because they understand us, and as long as they don't rock the boat they're alright by us.

The only problem with this scenario is that one need fight the *good fight* in order to lay hold of eternal life, and in the end that is the motivation. That is the driving force of why we choose to enroll in God's army and do battle against the enemy.

Eternal life: the promise and the prize. The reward for your faithfulness, exertion, sweat, blood, tears, prayers, self-discipline, and everything else a life in Christ entails is eternal life.

It is not an earthly reward, it is not some material thing that rusts and loses luster with time; it is eternal life with God in His kingdom forever.

Once we understand the magnitude of what we're fighting for, the training, the equipping, the exhaustion and the bruises are all worth it. Every scar, every blister, every sleepless night, every single one is more than worth it when we acknowledge the reality of what God offers as reward to those who overcome, and remain faithful until the end.

> Revelation 3:21, "To him who overcomes I will grant to sit with Me on My throne, as I also overcame and sat down with My Father on His throne."

Not only does inheriting eternal life require we fight the good fight, it stipulates we must win the battle. We must overcome for *to him who overcomes* will Christ grant to sit with Him on His throne.

Men can twist it however they want. They can give their spin and put their personal interpretation on it – insisting that Jesus didn't really say what He in fact said – but the verse is there, plainly written, so even the plainest of men can understand it. The honor to sit with Christ on His throne is reserved for those who overcome.

It is not our duty to get along with the devil. It is not our duty to make peace with the enemy. It is not our duty to try and explain away God's righteousness and holiness. It is our duty to defend the Gospel, if need be with our lives, and stand for truth even if we happen to be the only one standing before a sea of men.

I realize full well that some of us do not see ourselves in this role. That's fine, neither did Gideon. What we must understand, what we must allow to sink deep into our marrow and take root in our hearts is that we must be willing, and God will do the rest.

He will strengthen us when the time comes if we are faithful and true. He will strengthen us when the time comes if we stand in Him no matter what. It's not that those who came before us were braver men than we. It's not that those who came before us were cut from a different cloth. Those that came before us were committed plain and simple. They were committed because they knew what they were fighting for down to the very fiber of their being, and they would not allow forked tongued fools to sway them in their convictions.

They had purposed in their hearts to remain faithful no matter what, and seeing the sincerity of their heart, seeing their desire to remain faithful, God strengthened them and equipped them to the point that they remained faithful even unto death.

Thankfully, we weren't just thrown upon this spinning rock and left to fend for ourselves. God is with us as long as we are with Him, and He will defend, protect, strengthen, and comfort us every time we need it.

Does this mean that we will never be called upon to endure hardship? Does this mean that we will never be called upon to endure persecution? Does this mean that we will never be called upon to suffer, and perhaps even die for the cause of Christ? No, the fact that God will be with us means none of those things.

What it does mean, what it has always meant since the advent of persecution against the saints, is that God will give the necessary strength and fortitude to weather every storm. He will give the necessary wherewithal to stand no matter who the foe happens to be, and He will give the peace surpasses all understanding in our darkest hour.

Do not be afraid. Stand firm, and be committed to defending the truth and righteousness of God.

The life of a soldier is not an easy one. The Word of God forewarns us that if we desire to be soldiers of Jesus Christ, we will have to endure hardships, we will have to be molded, matured, refined, trained, and battle tested, because all these are necessary steps to making a true soldier.

Not only does a pretend soldier pose a danger to their own person because they are untrained, ill equipped, and likely fearful of the enemy's advances, the pretend soldier is a danger to those around him as well. Much of the time a pretend soldier serves as a distraction for the true soldiers, because what they are doing is so out of step with what ought to be done, that even the most seasoned warrior is surprised by their actions.

Yes, I know, we like to tell each other God is doing something new all the time, so it's perfectly fine if some knucklehead is kicking cancer patients in the stomach, but in reality such individuals are a distraction, and oftentimes a source of shame for the household of faith because of their actions.

It's one thing to suffer for righteousness' sake, it's quite another to suffer due to the actions of some conman whom the world automatically associates with you because he calls himself a Christian just as you do.

I've been asked on a number of occasions to come alongside other ministries, to validate certain preachers, to lend my name to some gathering or another, and I've always been hesitant because I know once I lend my name to a certain event or individual I will be associated with them for better or worse.

This is the reason I do not endorse ministers by and large. If I do endorse, it is only after I possess enough knowledge about them, as brothers or sisters in Christ, to ascertain that they are walking the walk and not just talking the talk.

The Bible tells us our God changes not. He remains the same in perpetuity, and if something worked perfectly well a thousand years, a hundred years, or a day ago, God is wise enough not to mess with it, or try to improve upon it. How can one improve upon perfection? How can one improve upon something God Himself created and put together?

Yes, men take it upon themselves to try and help God, to improve the ways and means by which we reach out to the lost, or attract the world to the household of faith, but these are gimmicks God neither sanctioned nor approved. We do these things of our own volition, driven by our own vanity, unimpeded in our actions by the reality that God is not in it.

So what does this have to do with knowing what you're fighting for? No matter what motivates you to battle, no matter what you're fighting for, fighting in defense of the truth will always be undergirding this motivation.

In the end that's what it comes down to. We fight against the darkness, we fight against deception, we fight against principalities and powers, we fight against the rulers of the darkness of this age, we fight against spiritual hosts of wickedness in heavenly places, and as reward for our service we receive a crown.

It's as important to know what you are fighting against as to know what you are fighting for. Some men are zealous in their desire to do battle, but they have not a clue against whom they battle. Rather than identify and pursue the enemy, rather than strike out at the darkness, they end up fighting amongst themselves, wounding both brothers and sisters alike, because they had not the discipline to grow, and understand who their battle was with.

It is important to go through basic training. It is important to be taught war. It is important to possess the ability to identify your enemy. It is important to know what you are fighting for. It is important to know how to wield the weapons in your arsenal, so that when war does come, you are prepared, you are ready, and rather than flee from before the enemy, you will advance against him as a true warrior ought.

Just consider this: God even allowed certain enemies of Israel to remain in the olden days, simply so the children of Israel might be taught war.

> *Judges 3:1-3, "Now these are the nations which the Lord left, that He might test Israel by them, that is, all who had not known any of the wars in Canaan (this was only so that the generations of the children of Israel might be taught to know war, at least those who had not formerly known it), namely, five lords of the Philistines, all the Canaanites, the Sidonians, and the Hivites, who dwelt in Mount Lebanon, from Mount Baal Hermon to the entrance of Hamath."*

We cannot shy away from battle, nor can we shy away from the training implicit in every soldier's life so that he might be able to not only defend himself, but advance into enemy territory and vanquish him.

God did not want His people to forget what war was like, nor did he want them to forget what being a soldier implied, so He allowed certain nations to remain for this specific reason.

Nowadays we've come to believe that just because our fathers knew spiritual warfare, it is enough. Since they knew it, in our mind there is no need for us to know it, not realizing that every generation and every individual must stand on the battle field, and on that day all that will matter is whether or not you've learned warfare, or just pretended at it.

History is rife with individuals who counted on their pedigree to see them through, only to find themselves fleeing from before their enemy in fear.

Thankfully, I don't have a reputation to protect, or a following to impress, or a demographic to win over to my side, so I can still tell you the truth whether it hurts or soothes. That is what soldiers do. They do the work. They do the hard tasks. Soldiers run into the battle, they put on their armor, and they stand for what they know they ought to stand for, sometimes knowing full well that it's only a matter of time before they are either injured or killed.

In order to be willing to lay your life down, in order to consciously make the choice to forfeit your dreams, aspirations, expectations, and future you must know, and vividly so, the driving force and the motivation behind this decision.

Every man and woman of God throughout history has known what it was they were fighting for. Everyone, to the last, who has left their mark, who is remembered, who stood out from the pack in their bravery and valor, knew why they were doing it. It takes a certain level of self-awareness and intimate knowledge of God to choose to remain faithful, knowing that it will mean nevermore seeing another sunrise.

When we do not know what we are fighting for, when we are not certain of our motivation, we are easily swayed, readily silenced, and far too often made to flee from before the enemy. Thoughts begin to creep in, and sooner than one might think we find justification for desertion and excuses for cowardice.

The flesh is ever ready to supply us with a long list of why we shouldn't stand, why we shouldn't fight, and why it's best to keep our head down. The flesh is ever ready to try and save itself, keep itself comfortable for as long as possible and spare itself hardship of any kind.

The enemy knows that if he can get into your head, if he can make you doubt your calling, if he can make you doubt your motivation, if he can make you doubt the need for battle, he's gained the upper hand even before the first blow is struck.

The devil's desire is to face you at your weakest, not at your strongest. His desire is to make you doubt, because doubt is the fertile ground in which the defeatist mentality can grow unencumbered.

Even if during the battle you have moments of doubt or moments when you feel your strength ebbing, although you have identified what you are fighting and it is well defined and preeminent in your actions, you will fight through the doubt, you will fight through the exhaustion and weariness because your goal is worth the effort.

Only you know what you are fighting for. Make certain that it is something that will sustain you throughout, something that will keep you advancing on the enemy and doing your utmost to vanquish him.

If your motivation is not strong enough you will give up the fight sooner rather than later because an unmotivated soldier will do his utmost to avoid the frontlines of battle. Rather than make war against the darkness, a compromised soldier's utmost desire becomes to keep himself from toil, even abandoning his post if need be.

CHAPTER THREE

HOW FAR ARE YOU WILLING TO GO?

Now that you know what you are fighting for, the next logical question is, how far are you willing to go in order to attain that for which you are fighting? What is your faith costing you today? Would you remain faithful if it cost you twice as much tomorrow? Would you remain faithful still if the day after it cost you twice as much again?

What if instead of dirty looks once in a while you were physically assaulted? What if instead of just feeling out of place at the mall your faith could cost you your life? How far are you willing to go? This is the question few believers today are willing to answer honestly because we've had it too good for too long, and we've conveniently chosen to ignore the fact that others are dying for the cause of Christ every day in this world of ours.

We are either involved or we are uncommitted. We are either aware that once enlisted in God's army we are no longer our own and as such must obey Him without equivocation, or we pretend at soldiering and go our own, easy way. On the fateful day, though, when the enemy stands before the pretenders grinning and merciless, with no defense to speak of, they will find themselves staring at an end that was a foregone conclusion the instant they decided to treat the things of God lightly.

As with any engagement there are rules and principles governing the battle we are currently engaged in, and the first of these has to do more with us as individuals than with the battle itself.

It is a principle which governs both physical and spiritual warfare, and that is total commitment to the objective at hand.

If you plan on being a duplicitous soldier with a divided heart, you might as well just stay off the battlefield altogether. If you plan on obeying only those orders which suit you, then you might as well just walk away now.

There can be no half-hearted commitment when it comes to this battle, just as there cannot be half-hearted commitment when it comes to battles in the physical.

Throughout history, some of the most protracted and fruitless wars have occurred because those in power were either not intent on winning, or were unwilling to do what it takes to win.

You begin a battle with the intent of winning, of overcoming, and vanquishing your enemy. You commit all resources, you deploy all available soldiers, you attack aggressively, because your purpose is not to be delicate, but to decisively win the battle as soon as possible. You know that for which you are fighting. The purpose is clear, the mission is clear, and the enemy before you has made himself known.

We cannot possess divided loyalties and still hope to be victorious in battle. We cannot possess divided loyalties and still hope to overcome the enemy. I guarantee you the enemy's loyalties are not divided. His purposes are not blurred, and his intent is not swayed.

It is a sad reality that most often the soldiers of the light are not as committed as the soldiers of the darkness when it comes to their objective. It is a sad reality that most often the enemy is more purposed in his intent than are the children of God. This is unfortunate, because knowing who our Father is, knowing who our General is, knowing who leads this great army into which we have been conscripted, we ought to be all the more valiant in the battle and purposed in our intent.

Try as we might, we can't get away with halfhearted commitment. We can't get away with just showing up but never putting on our armor, or putting on our armor but never drawing our sword. We show up to the battlefield ready and intent on confronting the enemy, as committed to our cause as he is to his, because we know the battle is for keeps. There will be no prisoners, and there will be no quarter given.

The devil isn't playing games, but sadly much of the church is. Tragically the devil understands the stakes of this battle far better than most believers, and it is this ignorance of the prize that keeps many from committing their all to the endeavor of standing against the enemy.

The darkness we are currently seeing spreading across the globe, the increase in despair, the increase in wickedness, the increase in the vile practices of vile individuals, is all due to the Church's failure to stand its ground and defend the truth. What we are seeing, all of it, the darkest most heinous parts of what man is capable of, is what happens when evil goes unchecked and no one is willing to stand up and confront it.

We cannot bemoan the current spiritual climate if we never once stood in defense of Jesus. We cannot bemoan the current spiritual climate if we never once stood in defense of truth. Our inaction has birthed the monsters we are now forced to stare down. Our inaction has birthed the wickedness threatening to choke off the household of faith.

To think that just because you are living in America you will never be called upon to stand for your faith is foolishness at best, and outright madness at worst. The days will come, and perhaps sooner than any of us think, wherein many will have to stand for what they believe in, and the standing will cost them something, perhaps everything.

If we are not wholly committed to the cause of Christ now, when no one is putting a gun to our head, when no one is threatening us with certain death, what makes us think we will muster up the courage to be valiant when it does happen?

If in your heart you are uncertain about your commitment, if as yet you do not know how far you are willing to go, then you are not yet willing to go all the way. Anything except purposing in one's heart to remain faithful unto death is a cheap excuse that will fall the instant the slightest pressure is applied.

I realize full well the enablers of spiritual impotence within God's house will have a field day with my previous assertions, calling them unloving and intolerant, but if they don't love you enough to tell you the truth, let that be on their own head. I cannot but pour out my heart and tell you all that I know concerning being battle-ready. What you do with it is entirely up to you.

There is a reason we are commanded to put on the *full* armor of God. There is a reason are commanded to gird up the loins of our mind, and it all has to do with how far we are willing to go when confronted with the notion that we might have to go all the way.

You never know when your moment will come. You never know when you will be called upon to stand for the name Jesus, and if you are doubleminded, if your heart is divided, if you are attempting to walk the fine line between God and Mammon, you will fail the test, and you will deny the Christ as Peter did.

If you think you'll never have to stand for the name Jesus because you are not an elder, think again. If you think you'll never have to stand for the name Jesus because you're not a deacon, a preacher, an evangelist, a pastor, or a minister, think again.

On a good day I tend to think that those who insist upon the idea that God is perfectly fine with spiritual slothfulness are just well meaning if misguided. On a bad day I tend to think they are the devil's pawns, and the entirety of their duty is to keep the household of faith at ease, unprepared, and spiritually stunted.

We didn't want to scare folks so we watered down what it means to be a believer. We made the conscious choice to hide, or at least camouflage, the reality that we are at war. *Soldiering is for soldiers* we told everyone and anyone who would hear, neglecting to mention that they too were soldiers in the army of God if they named the name of Christ.

Nobody started out being a soldier. Throughout the Word of God, we see average, everyday individuals with wide ranging skills, from shepherding to wheat threshing, being conscripted into the army of God, and becoming legends whose names live to this day.

The one commonality all the memorable warriors of the Bible shared was wholehearted commitment to God, a willingness to lay down their lives, and a desire to see the glory of God made manifest in their lives.

Gideon was threshing wheat in a winepress away from the prying eyes of the Midianites when the angel of the Lord appeared to him calling him a mighty man of valor, or valiant warrior.

At the moment the angel first met Gideon he was neither valiant nor mighty, yet the story of Gideon proves out that eventually. He became both. Gideon was able to grow into the man the angel of the Lord had described him as, because no matter what the circumstances, no matter the cost, no matter the opposition, his desire was to serve the Lord with all that he was. Gideon would allow no compromise in his life. This underlying foundation of faithfulness is what matured Gideon into one of the most legendary warriors within the pages of Scripture.

From the first command God gave him, Gideon obeyed. When God commanded him to tear down Baal's altar – even though he proceeded to do it at night for fear of what his father's household and the men of the city would do – he followed through and did the hard thing.

To us, what God asked of Gideon might seem like an easy thing, but when taking into account that the people had abandoned the one true God for Baal and had surrendered their hearts to him, it is not an intellectual leap to conclude that Gideon would have likely been murdered had he been caught destroying the idol of Baal.

Gideon followed through with God's command even though he knew it may well cost him his life. He followed through with God's command fully willing to accept any blowback and consequence for having carried out his obedience.

When we are fully engaged in carrying out our obedience in the present, we are no longer made fearful by the consequences of our action in the future. What I mean by this is, rather than twist myself into knots as to how someone will react if I begin a conversation about Jesus, I just begin the conversation. The immediacy of obedience does a lot to dispel nagging fear, and altogether does away with second guessing of oneself.

If the Holy Spirit stirs me to share Jesus with someone, if I start analyzing all the ways they might react – wondering if they will be offended or worse – my window may well close, I may well lose my opportunity, and by delaying my obedience, I may have just missed out on seeing a move of God, and a soul brought to the light of truth.

Sometimes there is wiggle room as far as timing is concerned, as we saw with Gideon. He delayed tearing down Baal's idol until night came, but in many instances the need for us to obey and follow through with a stirring from the Spirit is time sensitive and requires immediate action.

Once he completed the task of tearing down Baal's idol the people of the city were so irate that they began to investigate who could have done such a thing. Finally, Gideon's game surfaced, and sure enough, they showed up at his father's door asking that Gideon be sent out that he might die.

Gideon understood the inherent risk in tearing down the altar of Baal. He was under no delusion that he could destroy his countrymen's place of worship without fallout or recrimination. Having lived his entire life in his father's house, and understanding that there really are no secrets in a small community, he also understood that eventually he would be found out.

Gideon also understood he could not count on his father's clout or ability to protect him, because by his own admission his family was the least in Manasseh. It's not as though his family was feared. It's not as though once he destroyed the altar of Baal he was certain of sanctuary in his father's house.

When you stack up all the negative ramifications tearing down Baal's idol would have had for Gideon, it was only his total commitment that steeled him, and compelled him to follow through with the command God gave him.

Sometimes God will ask you to do the hard thing. Sometimes God will ask you to do something that might seem downright impossible to human reason. No matter what He asks, if He asked it of you it is within your purview and ability to do it. The only unknown factor in the equation remains your wherewithal, and your willingness to go beyond your comfort zone, beyond what you think impossible, to the realm of absolute trust in God.

It is in this realm, the realm of absolute trust that we begin to see the supernatural power of God aiding us in our quest, and giving us the boldness to go beyond what we think ourselves capable of doing.

No matter how strong you may think yourself to be, it takes divine courage to affirm Christ in the face of death without hesitation. It's not as though those who are confronted with making the ultimate sacrifice for Jesus are given days to weigh everything, to analyze and reason out, then come to a conclusion. It is a split second decision, something which you must already know as absolute truth in your heart long before you are confronted with the choice.

There are some who insist that they could make their minds up on the spot, once confronted with the situation, if such a drastic situation ever arises. They reason to themselves that the odds of having to stand, perhaps even die for one's faith are negligible, and so they need never determine in their hearts how far they are willing to go for the cause of Christ.

Although such justifications might sound reasonable on the surface, the truth of the matter is that anyone unwilling to honestly assess where they stand and how far they are willing to go for Jesus has already answered the question in a roundabout way.

The only reason to put off assessing how far you are willing to go is because in your heart of hearts you already know you are not willing to go all the way. The only reason to beat around the bush and come up with excuses for not knowing whether you are willing to lay down your life for the cause of Christ is because you are, as yet, unwilling to do so.

People don't put off doctor's exams because they know they are healthy and their tests will come back declaring them at the peak of their physicality. Even though very few are willing to admit it, people put off going in for their checkup because they know something's off, something doesn't feel right, and the doctor will just confirm what they've been suspecting all along.

Ignorance of a fact does not nullify the fact. Facts are facts whether we acknowledge them or not. They are inescapable realities which we must either confront and deal with, or attempt to avoid until avoidance becomes impossible.

It is a far better thing to know where you stand, to know what you are willing to sacrifice, to know how far you are willing to go, and make the necessary change while there is still time, than to find oneself put in the position of affirming or denying Christ only to deny Him because you had not counted the cost.

Certain things just cannot be delayed. Try as we might to put off an eye exam when we start seeing blurred images, eventually, when it gets bad enough, when we start bumping into things and petting the neighbor's Holstein as though it were a puppy, we will have no choice but to go in and see how close to blindness we really are. Try as we might to put off going to the doctor, when the discomfort gets unbearable and it just won't go away, eventually, given enough pain, we will do what would have saved us much pain had we done it earlier.

Today's modern, westernized church attendees are largely ineffective when it comes to the things of the Kingdom because their commitment is partial and not total. They know not what it is to die for Jesus, so living for Him is anathema as well. They know not what it is to count the cost, realize it will cost you everything, and still conclude that it is worth pursuing Christ with abandon given everything it will entail.

Yes, there are still some, handfuls of men and women here and there who live lives worthy of the name Jesus, who would affirm Him even in the face of death, but such individuals ought not to be the exception among the people of God.

The willingness to lay our lives down for the sake of Jesus ought to be common among Christians. It ought to be so often seen an occurrence that it would surprise no one, and come to be expected of those calling themselves believers.

One of the most sobering questions I ask myself on a regular basis is whether I am willing to go as far as Jesus is willing to take me. If my answer to this question is ever no, then I know it's time for me to walk away from ministry because from that moment onward I will be ineffective in my calling.

God cannot use those who are not willing to go all the way with Him. God cannot use those who will stop halfway through the journey in protest, demanding more possessions, more rest days, and more accolades from the world.

There is a pervasive myth making its way through the churches today insisting that God has no expectations of His servants, that there is no code of conduct one must adhere to, and that there are no sacrifices that need be made for the Kingdom of God. This myth has wormed its way into many a heart, and because it is so pleasing to the flesh it is widely accepted as Gospel, when it's the furthest thing from it.

Even the most rinky-dink, peanut gallery army in the world has a code of conduct that its soldiers must adhere to. Even the most rinky-dink, amateurish, military operation has guidelines, a command structure, and certain expectations of those who've enlisted.

What makes us think that the army of God has no such code of conduct? What makes us think that one can join the army of God with no reasonable expectation of service, but with all the benefits to which the enlisted are entitled?

Can you imagine the percentages of those who will eventually wash out of God's army simply because no one took the time to inform them that something was expected of them?

One cannot show up on the battlefield ready for slumber rather than battle and expect their commanding officer to be fine with it. One cannot fail to have a passing understanding of the weapons provided them and expect that there be no repercussions for their failure to grow.

Herein we see yet another danger of fraudulent, unscriptural, and heretical doctrine. Herein we see yet another danger of coddling the lukewarm rather than insisting that they be either hot or cold. Herein we see yet another reason modern Christianity so minimally resembles Biblical Christianity, because rather than pray to be spared the Christians of old prayed for boldness, and rather than flee trials, tribulations, and persecutions, they embraced them and gloried in them.

What profit is there, either for oneself or for the army they've enlisted in, if they leave basic training with the same skills, same understanding, and same lack of discipline as when they first signed on?

If not all who say "Lord, Lord" will enter His kingdom, then it is safe to conclude that not all those who say they are soldiers in the army of God will ever be seen as such by Him.

We are told we must endure as faithful soldiers, not partway, not halfway, but to the end. If this truth has not been established in our hearts, then we will not be long for the battle.

In honestly answering how far you are willing to go, you will know whether or not you are battle-ready. You will know whether or not you are ready to be placed on the front lines, or require another season of maturing and growing in God.

Unlike the world's armies, God is not interested in cannon fodder. He is not interested in ill equipped, double minded, fearful soldiers with divided loyalties. God is not concerned with the number of soldiers in His army, but with the quality of the soldiers in his army.

He would rather you not show up on the battlefield at all than to see you abandon your post and retreat halfway through the battle. When one has not determined how far they are willing to go, they are easily swayed and dissuaded the instant difficulty arises and the going gets tougher than they expected it to get.

Will you still stand when the cost of standing is more than just an insult or a bruised ego? Will you stand when the cost of standing is more than just losing a friendship or the loss of career advancement? Will you stand when the cost of standing isn't one thing but everything?

Determine how far you are willing to go and establish it in your heart. If how far you are willing to go isn't all the way, then systematically begin to remove those things you hold dear above Jesus in your life until He reigns supreme on the throne of your heart. It is the only way one can truly be battle-ready and stand their ground when the day of battle comes.

A positive attitude, mantras, daily affirmations, or a glowing self-image will do nothing to strengthen or embolden you when the enemy is standing inches away, his intent clear and undeniable in his countenance.

The world as we know it has changed dramatically over the course of just a few short years. This change will not only continue to take place, it will accelerate dramatically, and as such, things some never thought possible in their lifetime will become all too common.

One of the things we must fully expect, even in bastions of illusory freedom such as America, is persecution against Christians. The noose is already tightening, the saints of God are already being corralled, but as yet the only pressure brought to bear is either economic or emotional. History has proven time and again that it is but one small step to go from economic pressure to physical pressure, because in the eyes of the godless the handful of souls still standing for truth are, in fact, standing in the way of progress.

Because you cling to Jesus, because you cling to your Bible, you are branded a hindrance, an obstacle that must either be surmounted or removed. The minds of many have so been seared that permanent removal seems like a far easier and more economical way to go than trying to surmount the issue of Christians and their pesky absolutes, and they will have no qualms about committing the most inhuman of acts in order to save humanity. Although these words might seem doom-laden in the present, the truth of them will be evident in the not too distant future.

In light of the expectation with which we as believers are living, it is only prudent and wise, it is only practical and judicious that we determine the lengths to which we are willing to go for our faith, and the sacrifice we are willing to make for the name Jesus.

CHAPTER FOUR

ARE YOU MATURE ENOUGH?

There are baby Christians and there are immature Christians. This chapter is meant for the latter rather than the former. You can still work with a baby Christian, guide them in the ways of the Lord and watch them grow into a mature, well equipped, valiant warrior of the faith. The baby Christian is not the problem. The problem, as I see it, is that there are fully grown adult men and women walking about who've been attending church since they were teenagers, and they are as immature today as the first day their shadow fell across the entryway of the church they walked the aisle in.

The question ought not to be whether God can still do what He says He can do in His Word. The question ought not to be whether God will keep up His end of the bargain. The question ought not to be whether or not He is everything He claims to be. If we are intellectually honest we all know He can, He will, and He is!

The question ought to be whether you are mature enough to do what you aspire to do and still remain humble. The question ought to be whether you are spiritually mature enough to handle the gifts for which you have been petitioning God, but I get ahead of myself.

Mention spiritual maturity to some, and they will react as though you've happened upon a sinister and taboo topic. From the squirming in their seats, to the rolling of the eyes, to the checking of their mobile devices, indifference toward the topic of spiritual maturity is plainly evident in many a congregation. While some are indifferent toward spiritual maturity, others consider it a topic for the elders of the church, the evangelists, the preachers, and those in leadership. In any case it's not for them, and when asked about it they will make their feelings very clear.

In order to achieve spiritual maturity sacrifice is required of the individual, and too many consider throwing some loose change in the offering plate every service as sacrifice enough. Spiritual maturity comes about through experience. It comes about through having lived a spiritual life, having fought the good fight, having been bruised, having been wearied, and having found comfort and healing at the foot of the cross. Spiritual maturity cannot be taught; it must be lived.

Contrary to popular belief, spiritual maturity is not reserved only for the select few in leadership. It is a requirement and necessity for every individual who has yoked themselves to Christ. It is mandatory for everyone who has begun their journey toward perfection, sanctification, and the deeper mysteries of God.

Just as growing and maturing physically is a natural process of this present life, so is growing and maturing spiritually. When one remains in a state of spiritual infancy, they become easy prey for the wolves and the enemy that roam about.

The Word warns us repeatedly both of the enemy's devices, but also of those individuals in whom there is no light or truth, and who are actively looking for their next victim, the next soul they can corrupt, and the next heart they can defile.

The Word continually encourages us to grow, to pursue the deeper things, to ascend from grace to grace and from glory to glory. Our journey is a process wherein we are weaned off milk and begin to consume solid food. As we grow we begin to hear the voice of God for ourselves, understand the Word for ourselves, and eventually stop relying on surrogates to nourish us spiritually.

Many a soul should be further along in their spiritual maturity than they are, and the constant reaffirmations by some in Christian leadership that growth is not necessary, is largely to blame for this spiritually underdeveloped generation.

In his letter to the Hebrews, Apostle Paul addressed just such a deficiency and lack of spiritual maturity. He reproved them for their lack of growth, and for their need to continue consuming milk rather than solid food.

Hebrews 5:12, "For though by this time you ought to be teachers, you need someone to teach you again the first principles of the oracles of God; and you have come to need milk and not solid food."

Childhood is beautiful. The carefree days spent doing trivial things, the wonder of it all as we discover the world beyond our front door, the excitement of the first day of school, the rush of our first schoolyard tussle. The list goes on and on. The memories grow muted the further along we sail down the river of life, the sense that each new day was a new chapter, which held a new discovery and a new experience, dissipating a little more with each new moon.

As all things temporal must, the season of our childhood passes. We are children for the blink of an eye, then comes the part time job, then the full time job, marriage, mortgages, car loans, pension plans and family doctors. A child cannot remain a child forever. One cannot be forever young, forever carefree, forever absent of responsibility or maturity.

If one remains in a constant state of infancy, eventually the parents grow worried, concerned, perturbed, and seek help realizing something is very wrong. The child that should have grown hasn't grown. He is not maturing at the same rate and speed as the others are, and this is a reason for concern for most parents.

Discipleship is necessary, but if its time passes and the disciple does not become skilled, if he is not well on his way to mastering his skill, it is all in vain; an exercise in futility. We are Disciples of Christ because our desire is to one day be like Him. The desire of every true believer is to one day be like His Master. We are daily formed, daily molded, daily chiseled, and daily matured, allowing the nature of Christ to take hold, to shine in us and through us.

This present life requires growth. Whether physical or spiritual, everyone must grow consistently and without fail. It is necessary, mandatory, and a natural law. If growth and progress are not found, if we become bogged down in a state of static existence wherein we are not moving forward in our faith, we can no longer hope to ascend to the greater things of God.

Only by spiritual growth are we entrusted with greater responsibility, greater power, greater revelation, and greater intimacy. A spiritually mature man or woman realizes the true value of their relationship with God and they nurture it, they protect it, being watchful not to allow any stumbling blocks to stand in the way.

A spiritually mature individual prepares for battle, all the while praying that the battle never comes. A spiritually mature individual understands the price that must be paid in any war, but also perceives the danger in not standing to fight. Above all, a spiritually mature individual is balanced, neither itching for a fight, nor retreating from one.

A spiritually mature soul has gone beyond the first principles of the oracles of God. They have laid the foundation, and now they are building the temple. One must learn the first principles first, but always strive to grow beyond the first principles of the oracles of God. One cannot bypass the first principles and hope to gain instant understanding of the deeper mysteries of God.

One cannot bypass basic training and hope to lead a battalion into battle. A soldier's mettle is tested before they are given the responsibility of leading others onto the battlefield. A soldier's skill, aptitude, and ability must all be tested before he is deemed fit for warfare, and no matter how much we may try to insist otherwise, it will not change the truth of it. As the old adage states, first things, always come first.

In many instances we can view our spiritual growth as a ladder. One cannot climb to the top of the ladder unless he has started out on the bottom rung. Each rung of the ladder has its own relevance and its own importance because with each step we take we ascend higher to our desired goal. Many souls climb the first few rungs and then settle comfortably, thinking there are no more rungs to the ladder. Three feet off the ground and some already believe they've ascended to the highest highs of God's wisdom, knowledge, and glory.

By adopting the mindset that we have already attained when we have not attained, that we have already achieved when we have not achieved, we grow complacent, stagnant, indifferent, and great only in our own eyes. When such a mindset worms its way into a heart, said heart quickly becomes unreachable, for one who already believes he knows all there is to know can no longer be taught.

It becomes a chain reaction of events that lead up to the sin of pride springing up in the heart, and we become blinded by our own self-proclaimed genius, no longer willing to take direction even if that direction happens to come directly from the Word of God.

We draw up our own battle plans even though they might contradict God's battle plans, and we rush headfirst into a battle of our choosing without the advantage of having God standing beside us.

Many believers suffer defeat at the hands of the enemy because the battle they were engaged in was not sanctioned by God. Many believers suffer defeat at the hands of the enemy because rather than wait patiently for their marching orders, they go off half-cocked, thinking that they are doing God a favor by taking the initiative.

Though many ought to be warriors by now, their own self-destructive tendencies and the pride, which they allowed to take root in their hearts, makes them need to reacquaint themselves with the training manual, and perhaps go through basic training once more.

Though many ought to be teachers by now, their unwillingness to submit to the authority of Scripture and humble themselves makes them need milk once more rather than solid food, and makes it necessary for them to reacquaint themselves with the basic principles, and first oracles of God.

A spiritual walk has its own natural progression. Spiritual growth comes about naturally when we humble ourselves and strive to grow in God. It is the Father's good pleasure to see us grow and mature, to see constancy in our spiritual journey. In order to attain what He has for us, we must become what He desires us to be.

A Christian who has remained in a state of spiritual infancy is not troubled by the sin in his life. He has as yet not come to realize the dangers of sin just as a baby has not realized the dangers of touching a hot stove, or sticking its fingers in the wall socket. There are certain things we perceive only when we are older, just as there are spiritual matters we perceive only when we have matured spiritually.

One lacking spiritual maturity is readily adamant in defending their doctrine or theology, even if it contradicts the Scripture. Pride does not allow them to see the truth, and so they press on in their ignorance attempting to bring others to their way of thinking.

The telltale signs of an immature Christian are plentiful and easy to detect if one knows what they are looking for.

The life of an immature Christian is a life of defeats, absent of peace, absent of balance, and absent of joy. An immature Christian cannot overcome, for they trust in their own strength. They cling to the notion that the battle is won in the physical and not the spiritual, and they do their utmost to influence the plan and will of God rather than submit to it. They have, as yet, not surrendered themselves in their entirety to the will of God, and inevitably suffer the consequences of disobedience.

Romans 7:20, "Now if I do what I will not to do, it is no longer I who do it, but sin that dwells in me."

One who is spiritually immature does not possess the fruit of the Spirit. They are a barren tree producing no fruit. The spiritually immature soul is always helped along and learning from others, never coming to the knowledge of truth on their own. There are always in need of crutches, security blankets, surrogates, for they are unable to consume solid food.

Because they live lives of dependency upon others, the spiritually immature also tend to idolize those to whom they turn for spiritual succor. As such, for many, even when their spiritual mentors begin to teach things contrary to Scripture, they will either overlook it or somehow justify it until the moment it becomes such an overshadowing issue they are forced to either break ties and repent, or knowingly believe a lie in lieu of the truth.

Another telltale sign of an immature Christian is that they are always suspicious. Immature Christians are always in pursuit of their own self-interest. They are in constant search of vainglory and choose not to see the good or the nobility in others. Their desire is only for themselves, their own honor and their own praise. As such, submitting to authority becomes difficult for them, and they will often go against the orders of their commanding officer if they feel it will benefit them somehow. Theirs is not a quest for the furtherance of the Kingdom of God. Theirs is a quest for the furtherance of the kingdom of self.

Is your desire His glory or your personal vainglory? Is your desire to serve Him unconditionally or do you hope to profit from your relationship with Him in some form or fashion? Is it all about Him or is it all about you? The answers to these questions will determine your effectiveness on the battlefield, and whether or not you will bring honor to Him by your endeavors.

The life of an immature Christian is also formulaic, formalistic and hypocritical. Rather than serve God, the immature believer uses God, as though He were some benevolent genie ready to grant every wish and desire of the heart. The interest of the immature Christian lies not in establishing a relationship or intimacy with the heavenly Father, but to profit from the acquaintance, feigning worship only inasmuch as it will aid them in achieving their desired result.

What I find interesting is that in his epistle to the Hebrews, Paul's first warning was concerning dangers of neglect, his second warning concerning the dangers of unbelief, and his third and final warning concerning the danger of not maturing. Once they have passed the first two hurdles in their spiritual journey, many souls succumb to the third, remaining in a state of spiritual infancy whereby they are unable to enter into the blessings of God, evermore unfit for duty, and dependent upon others. It is not enough to give earnest heed to the things we have heard, nor is it enough to believe. We must also grow in God, mature spiritually that we may ascend from being mere babes in Christ, to being soldiers for Christ.

Christ's physical and spiritual nature is a truth we learn as a first principle in the beginning of our walk with Him. To know him as our great High Priest, perpetually merciful and faithful, is a deeper truth we come to know only as we grow in God.

To know Him as our General, the One who not only gives us our marching orders but is leading the way into battle, is something we come to know only once we have completed our training, and are deemed ready to stand and fight.

There are many believers who are satisfied with the fact that they have received forgiveness of sins, that their conduct is somewhat better than those of the world, and that they have access to the eternal.

What more could a soul want? Is this not enough?

When we adopt the mentality that we can be satisfied in the knowledge we already retain, that we have traveled far enough wherein we can afford to take a break, to slumber a little, to rest of our weariness, we run the risk of losing everything.

To me the book of Hebrews is a cautionary tale. It is a warning to all who have spiritual ears to hear, that we ought not to grow lazy, slothful, indifferent, or satisfied; that we ought not to neglect so great a salvation. Ever onward should be our battle cry, and as faithful soldiers we ought not allow anything to keep us from growing in Christ.

Only by growing in knowledge and understanding can we perceive the beauty that is the deeper mystery of God. Only then can we begin to understand the full work of Christ's blood, not only on earth, but that it opened the doorway to heaven, to the eternal, wherein we can dwell in the holy place in constant fellowship with Him.

It is lamentable that having so much accumulated knowledge in our present generation concerning all that encompasses the Word, spirituality, theology, doctrine, the work of the Holy Spirit, and pretty much anything having to do with God, we still remain so ignorant concerning the greater things of God. It's not a lack of materials we suffer from, nor is it the lack of the Word for it is plentiful. It is lack of true desire and purpose to know the fullness of He who redeemed us from darkness and death.

Yes, by now we ought to be teachers. Yes, by now we ought to be soldiers. By now we ought to be ambassadors, and we ought to have the ability and desire to passionately tell others of the saving grace that is found in Christ Jesus. It is the duty of every believer to become a teacher, a confessor, a soldier, a light, a testimony, to be salt, an emissary of Christ here on earth. When the love of Christ fills a heart it does so to overflowing. The rarity with which we see the overflow in the lives of believers is shameful. That so many are content with the status quo, and so few desire more of God in their lives, is downright tragic.

It saddens God to see so many of His children dependent, waiting to be fed, and so few feeding others. It is a state of sickly infancy, of spiritual immaturity, and it is not beneficial to anyone. Most often this condition is allowed to perpetuate itself due to the false beliefs so many have concerning salvation, considering it only a selfish means of security, covering their bases just in case.

They never grow to know God in the intimate way He desires to be known. They never pursue or desire spiritual gifts, because all they really wanted was to know that they were getting into heaven. They raised their hand and said the sinner's prayer, and for far too many this is sufficient. It is enough. No more labor or sacrifice needed.

If our only reason for coming to God was to escape eternal punishment, if love does not overflow in our hearts and we feel no empathy for those who are lost in the world, we are still babes in Christ, in need of being taught again the first principles of the oracles of God.

If our focus is on self rather than the Kingdom, if our pursuit is ease and comfort rather than truth, then we have no place being on the battlefield, and a season of maturing is necessary. Immaturity will get you hurt, and far too often immaturity gets people killed. I know of people who have spent the better part of three decades trying to put their lives back together, trying to rediscover passion, trying to learn to trust again, all because in their spiritual immaturity they opened their hearts to things they ought not have, and it shipwrecked their faith altogether.

Hebrews 5:13, "For everyone who partakes only of milk is unskilled in the word of righteousness, for he is a babe."

Milk is an absolute necessity for a newborn. Without milk the life of the infant would not be possible. As necessary as milk might be in the beginning, it can also be equally dangerous if milk remains the only source of nourishment for a child that has grown past a certain age. Bread, meat, fruit and vegetables, must also be introduced into the diet, so that the child may grow and reach their full potential.

As of the writing of this book my wife and I have a sixteen month old daughter. As such, I was able to see firsthand the progressive stages of her diet, from exclusively feeding on mother's milk, to beginning to eat blended purees, to more solid foods, to finger foods, and eventually to watching her feed herself. One thing I noticed is that at first she didn't want to try anything different other than the milk she was used to. It was only after protracted insistence that she finally consented to eating something other than milk.

Believers are often similar in their reaction to more solid spiritual food. They know milk, they like milk, they are comforted by milk, and the thought of eating something other than milk gives them panic attacks at the drop of a hat. A true shepherd will insist upon the need for the meat of God's Word, and will do so until the babe realizes that as long as they only partake of milk they will remain unskilled in the word of righteousness.

From a spiritual perspective the aforementioned verse leads us to believe that the righteousness of God, as well as the other mysteries of God, cannot be understood by the babe in Christ. One who has only begun their spiritual journey, who is in their spiritual infancy, must nourish themselves with the milk of God's word until they are able to consume solid foods.

It is essential that the spiritual man is weaned off milk and begins to consume meat. It is essential that one matures beyond being taught to fight, to actually taking up the sword and the shield and doing some fighting. If after years and years of spiritual infancy there is no growth, the spiritual man remains vulnerable and defenseless. His life in Christ is unsure.

The righteousness of God is perceived and understood only by those who continue in their spiritual growth, who learn to mature their spiritual senses, and who listen for the voice of God. Far too many believers complain about not hearing the voice of God only to admit that they've never listened for it in the first place.

For too long we have been taught a one-dimensional spirituality wherein the potential for growth is nonexistent, and have been dulled into believing that within the span of a few spare minutes one can eternally ensure their salvation. The babe is unskilled in the word of righteousness, and does not realize the complexity and beauty that is this journey of faith toward eternity.

One can readily see the difference between the babe in Christ and one who has achieved maturity in Him, by how they perceive the Word of God. For some, the Bible remains a collection of stories with interesting characters and unbelievable events, while for those who have journeyed deeper into the mysteries of God it is life, it is light, it is breath, and it is the infallible, absolute Word of the omnipotent Father. You can tell a man's level of spiritual maturity or lack thereof by how he views the Bible, and the contents thereof.

God's desire for us as His children is to be skilled in the word of righteousness, to rightly discern between good and evil, and understand the marked difference between light and darkness. We pursue the good, we pursue the sovereign, we pursue sanctification and righteousness because we have reached the understanding that allows us to see it is the only way into the holy of holies. A child cannot judge rightly because he does not have the necessary maturity. A child has not reached the age wherein he can naturally discern between that which is righteous, and that which is defiled.

The consumption of milk is attractive to many who do not desire a deeper walk with God. They are content with being spoon fed for their entire spiritual journey because they never have to contend with finding nourishment for themselves. One grows disturbingly comfortable with the idea that a third party is responsible for their knowledge and understanding of God, for their spiritual succor, and for their protection, and those who would profit and take advantage of the babes in Christ love to have it so.

The sad and undeniable reality is that the wolves have always outnumbered the true shepherds. The only shift in the paradigm of late is that the sheep gravitate toward the wolves more than to the shepherds in greater numbers than ever before.

The wolves are easy to spot if you know what to look for. Most often they will not speak of the deeper things of God for fear of arousing the interest or the desire of the listening audience to get deeper into the Word for themselves. They will oftentimes speak in generalities, focusing on this present life. They will go on and on about the struggles of the flesh, about prosperity and self-esteem but remain utterly silent on those things which make us unique and set apart, those things which ought to define us as children of God.

If our focus is only on the things of this earth, on the wants and needs of this present life, if our goal is only to accumulate and hoard material possessions, then we are no different than the world. What's worse is that we will be held accountable for the fact that we ought to have known better, we ought to have sought out the things of God, we ought to have hungered for the meat of God's Word rather than be content with milk served from the pap of today's trendsetter pulpits.

There is nothing more tragic than an emaciated, malnourished soldier who is underequipped for the task at hand, and who has no clear directive from his commanding officer.

One of the surefire way to break the back of your adversary's advances is to compromise his supply line. If his soldiers can't eat, then they don't have the strength and the energy to fight, and if they have no strength and energy to fight, they will surrender at the first opportunity they are given.

The enemy is not ignorant of battle tactics. The enemy is not ignorant of what he needs to do in order to disrupt the forward momentum of God's army, and he has been about the task of disrupting the supply line of the household of faith for many a decade now.

What else would you call the onslaught of false doctrine being systematically introduced into the church? What else would you call the onslaught of heresy being passed off as gospel truth? What else would you call the compromised teachings of compromised men who have sold their souls for baubles and trinkets?

Getting beyond the stage of being merely babes in Christ and partaking only of milk is not an option but a necessity. Either we grow in God, we mature into self-sufficient soldiers sure of our right standing with God, certain of our foundation in Him, grounded in truth and righteousness, or we are trampled underfoot by the legions of darkness and the minions of deception.

Christianity has never been, nor will it ever be, a spectator sport. All must choose a side. All must either stand or fall, be resolute and steadfast in their faith, or blow away with the whirlwind.

The babes among us are the most susceptible to attack. They are the weak ones upon which the enemy preys incessantly. Those strong in their faith, those who have gone beyond the milk drinking stage must do their utmost to encourage those who are spiritually weaker than themselves to grow, to mature, and to pursue God with a singular passion and a singular desire.

Many today have the tendency to dismiss those who are in their spiritual infancy, not taking the time to disciple them, to grow them in the Word, to bring them to a place where they can feed themselves. If the love of God lives in our hearts, we must do as Christ did and reach out to all who cry out for help, and who seek to know God in greater measure but as yet have not discovered the means to do so. Selfish Christianity is off-putting, and detested of God.

If you have no other agenda but the Kingdom, if you have no other desire than to see men brought to Christ, if you have no other aspiration than to point the way to the cross and the blood, God will stand with you and provide the means and opportunity for you to fulfill your calling, and to be a true ambassador for the Kingdom of heaven.

Hebrews 5:14, "But solid food belongs to those who are full of age, that is, those who by reason of use have their senses exercised to discern both good and evil."

While grown men can readily consume children's food, children are unable to consume food that was meant for adults. In an attempt to get my nephew to eat his pureed carrots, I have often taken a bite myself, making the requisite sounds, hoping to entice him to eat them. The same cannot be said for him taking a bite of my steak, because he has no teeth, is unable to chew it, and even if he somehow got it down it would most likely lead to stomachaches and other maladies. Spiritual nutrition is not interchangeable from adult to babe, just as physical food is not interchangeable.

The natural state of a child of God is growth in every area of their life be it understanding, knowledge, strength, power, gifts, or wisdom. All these things must grow in us and become evident all the more. Our one purpose is to assimilate ourselves to God and become more like He who birthed us. Our nature, our flesh, our desires, and our goals need to lessen, decrease, and eventually die out altogether so that His nature, His desire, His purpose for us, and His will in our lives may increase and grow.

This present existence is a perpetual becoming. When a man is born again, it is like the caterpillar which after a given period of time in a cocoon becomes a butterfly. Something most find off-putting becomes something beautiful. Something graceless and dull becomes something graceful with the capacity for flight. The biggest transformation is that of being born again from death to life, from darkness to light, but as we grow and progress in God, we are constantly transforming, becoming that which He desires us to be, a more perfect and willing vessel, a mirror image of His Son here on earth.

A child cannot perceive the mysteries of things with its mind. A child cannot achieve understanding on its own, and is always dependent upon others to teach and show them. My mother had to teach me not to approach a barking dog, not to stick my hand in the wood burning stove, to blow on hot soup, to excuse myself when I burp, and a myriad of other things that were the building blocks of my constitution. A child is carried along at the mercy of both man and elements, unable to assist in its own defense.

As one grows and matures, things begin to change drastically. A grown man is no longer dependent. A grown man is no longer at the mercy of others nor does he constantly need to be told what he can and cannot do. By constant exercise of his senses the grown man is able to discern both good and evil, he is able to make the conscious choice whether to embrace the light or the darkness.

That one achieves the desired results by continuous exercise and good nourishment is true of spiritual growth as it is physical. Sound doctrine and the constant exercise of our senses brings us to that point of being able to rightly discern, to know the heart of a matter, the nature of a thing and not be enticed by its outwardly appearance.

If you want to get better at any skill, you practice more. If you want to become more knowledgeable about a given subject, you study more. It's not complicated, it's not beyond man's capacity to perceive, but it does require us to reprioritize our lives and make our spiritual preparedness a priority of utmost urgency.

An immature soul – one who has not achieved the necessary level of spiritual maturity – toying with doctrine, is just as dangerous as a child playing with a loaded gun. It is often the case that the babes become impertinent just as children are often fond of doing. We live amidst a generation who is defiant, who is largely unwilling to submit to spiritual authority, thereby coming to a tragic end. The old saying that *a little learning is a dangerous thing* holds true. In fact, a little learning is almost as dangerous as a lot of ignorance.

What we thought we knew when we were younger turns out to be less substantial than previously affirmed as we get older. There needs to be that season of discipleship in the life of every believer. There needs to be that time wherein someone who has already gone through the infant stages and come out a mature servant of God, can guide and warn of the pitfalls. Until one is able to stand on his own spiritual feet and lead a life of holiness and obedience, he must be taught and nourished by others more mature than themselves.

The discernment of which Paul speaks in his epistle to the Hebrews is a necessary component of every spiritual life. Joy or unhappiness, peace or unease, life or death, are all contingent on our ability to discern that which is good from that which is destructive. Discernment is achieved only by the constant exercise of the senses. It does not come of its own accord; it does not come suddenly, completely, neatly wrapped and ready to use. It is achieved by a sustained and constant labor led by the Holy Spirit.

Every member of a spiritual being must be exercised unceasingly so that it may contribute to the life one desires to live in Christ. When one member of the body atrophies, when one organ does not function, as it should, the whole suffers. Whether it is the prayer life that has atrophied, the study of the word, the fasting, the discernment, the exercise of the gifts, one underperforming member affects the entire spiritual body of the believer.

The eye must see the path which God has laid out for it; the ear must recognize His voice; the mind must reject without pause that which is displeasing in the sight of God; the will must choose to do only the will of God. All things, all senses, all members, must work in accordance, in unity, that we may achieve spiritual maturity and true fellowship with God.

It is important for us to understand that our progress is not dependent upon our talents, our intellect, or our abilities, but on the faithfulness with which we endeavor to rightly discern every day of our lives, and remain under the constant and uninterrupted guidance of the Holy Spirit.

Truthfully, a clean conscience and a will surrendered in totality to God are more important and relevant than the most brilliant of minds when it comes to living a life in Christ, and being a valiant soldier in God's army. Earthly wisdom, diplomas and degrees may be a noble pursuit in the eyes of some, but a nobler pursuit still is obedience and surrender to the will of God.

When one endeavors to grow in God it eclipses all other endeavors, all other pursuits, and all other desires. What can be greater than achieving sanctification which is nothing less than fellowship with Christ in obedience? We must be steadfast and resolute in our stance that we will accept nothing less than all of what Christ has for us.

Hebrews 6:1-2, "Therefore, leaving the discussion of the elementary principles of Christ, let us go on to perfection, not laying again the foundation of repentance from dead works and of faith toward God, of the doctrine of baptisms, of laying on of hands, of resurrection of the dead, and of eternal judgment."

There comes a time in the life of every believer when they must leave behind the elementary principles of Christ, and endeavor to go on to perfection. Plowing a field and sowing the seeds is very useful, in fact necessary, but if one would continually repeat these two procedures throughout an entire summer – plowing and sowing again and again – there would be no harvest at the end of the season, for the seeds would never be allowed to take root, to grow, and to mature. They would not be given the necessary time to bear fruit.

Would not a man who having finished planting his field then begins anew and plants the field once more, then repeats the process over and over be considered a fool? Although he would have accomplished one of the necessary steps required for seeing a harvest, the continuous repetition of that step would doom the man to starving beside his field, never seeing the fruit of his labors, never seeing the end result that his work should have produced.

It would likewise be considered madness if after finishing the first grade, graduating successfully and having learned all there was to learn, a student would return to the same class, in the same grade, resuming it over and over again until he is old and frail.

The danger of not growing, maturing, graduating, or climbing ever higher is that one is resigned to perpetual spiritual infancy. Such a soul is readily beguiled, deceived, and tempted, for he is uncertain, has no foundation, and will believe almost anything if presented in the right light and with the requisite unrealistic promises.

One cannot leave behind the first rung of a ladder until he has first climbed it. How can we hope to reach the second, third and fourth rung, if we have not ascended past the first, or if we find the first rung so comfortable that we forget there is a climb to be had at all?

The ladder of godly truths was given to us by Christ through the Holy Spirit, that we may climb it rung by rung, thus reaching our desired objective: that of being a reflection of Christ, of adopting His nature, and clothing ourselves in His righteousness that we may be valiant defenders of truth, warriors for holiness, soldiers of the cross for whom this world holds no temptation.

It is a case of simple logic that one should not continually lay the foundation of a home over and over again, but when one begins to build a home, a foundation is necessary. Our foundation in the Word is that one thing upon which the rest of our spiritual home is built. It must be strong, balanced, and evenly spaced that it may withstand the weight of the brick and mortar placed upon it, so a solid home might be built upon a solid foundation. The same principle can be applied spiritually wherein it is pointless to continually lay the foundation of repentance, but by the same token, a spiritual home in Christ cannot be built until that foundation of repentance has been laid.

Countless Christians are so enthralled and excited by the idea of gifts and miracles, of prophecies and dreams that they attempt to bypass the first step, the laying of the foundation of repentance from dead works. As the saying goes, they swing for the fences their first day out, wanting to be the greatest and most gifted among the brethren. What they fail to understand is that without the foundation of repentance soundly and solidly built, there can be no gifts, no prophecies, no dreams and no miracles.

Unwilling to humble themselves, unwilling to return to the foot of the cross and experience true repentance, many open themselves up to counterfeit movements, counterfeit gifts, imitations of the real that require less sacrifice than the authentic. Imitations are cheaper for a reason, and though it may not be a tragedy that you bought a fake wallet or a fake purse, it is the greatest of tragedies when one buys into fake spirituality and counterfeit doctrine. They are damaging, destructive, they stifle the truth, and they blind the eyes, leading inexorably to destruction.

The spiritual life of every believer begins with the first principles of the oracles of God absent of which said life is impossible to lead. After the first principles of the oracles of God are firmly established in a heart, one must advance, make progress, grow spiritually, and climb higher. Static Christianity is dangerous. For some it is even a death sentence. We must always be moving, aspiring to greater things in God, and the higher we climb, the more we desire to know, to see, to experience in Him.

The first principles, the first truths, are still the truths of Christ, therefore they must be sought and received, allowed to take root in our hearts and bear good fruit. Even the most moving of poets, the most eloquent of speakers, and the most profound of writers had to begin their journey by learning the alphabet. Even the greatest of mathematicians had to begin by learning the multiplication table. Even the greatest of warriors was once a novice, untrained in the ways of battle and in the use of his arsenal.

Everything has a beginning; every journey begins with a first step. Once the alphabet or the multiplication table is learned there is no need to learn them again for they are already known. After learning the alphabet we learn words, then sentences, then sentence structure, punctuation and so on.

Once the multiplication table is learned we then proceed to fractions, algebra, calculus, and our knowledge base expands as far as we are willing to study, to learn, and to grow in it.

Once the basics of weapons training is learned, one can go on to learn tactics, guerilla warfare, specialize in weaponry, and pursue a host of other avenues related to being a better soldier, but first, the basics.

When we learn a new thing it does not mean that we unlearn those things that we learned before. The building blocks of knowledge and wisdom can be stacked one upon another throughout a life, and still there will be so much more to learn.

If an individual believes in God, believes in Christ, believes in the resurrection of the dead, why then should they constantly be told to believe? If they have repented of dead works, embraced Christ and turned their back on the world, evidently and undeniably severing ties with the flesh, why should they constantly be told to stop doing such and such a thing in perpetuity? They had ceased those practices long ago. They had moved beyond the stage of emptying oneself of self, and have arrived at the stage of being filled.

Our journey toward perfection requires spiritual growth. It peers into the deeper mysteries of God, the mystery of the body of Christ, the intimate knowledge of God's plans, that we may become vessels of honor which God can use.

True followers of Christ must first be disciples, students, and then grow into being teachers. We leave the discussion of the elementary principles of Christ, that we may go on to perfection, that we may become preachers and teachers of the Word, that we may in turn lead others to Christ and the path of repentance.

So what is repentance from dead works, or more specifically what are the dead works to which Paul is referring? In broad strokes, dead works are every practice, ceremony or tradition in our lives that were not birthed of God, which did not originate from Him and His Word. There is a segment of the Christian population that believes if only they follow a certain set of traditions, or practice a certain kind of ceremony, it will not only bring them closer to God, but ensure their eternal rest in Him.

Paul is warning vehemently by the power of the Holy Spirit that placing our trust in dead works is a recipe for disaster. Lighting a candle, kissing a wooden cross, and a myriad of other things are woeful substitutes for a relationship with God. The mature Christian knows that nothing can substitute intimacy with the heavenly Father. Nothing can take the place of fellowship with Him.

Some overlook this verse, and interpret *dead works* to be the sins of our past, the glaring moral failings such as drunkenness, adultery, theft, and deception but we must take into account that this epistle was written to those who had gone beyond repentance of their sins, and Paul is attempting to point out that they should now repent of their form of godliness. Another term for a form of godliness is *pretend* soldiering, something far too many within the church seem troublingly comfortable with.

There are many today who practice Christianity only for the sake of appearance. They pray only when someone is watching, they attend service only as a formality, and they read the Word without understanding it. In short, possessing a form of godliness, but denying the power thereof. They praise God with their lips but their hearts are cold as stone, never having known the warmth of His love. These are the dead works of which we must repent without delay, for putting off repentance leads to the hardening of the heart.

Repentance is a constant necessity in the life of the believer, not for the works of the past but for the shortcomings of the present. I have already repented of my past and no longer need to revisit it for once a sin has been repented of it is cast into the sea of forgetfulness. We are, however, imperfect creatures serving a perfect God, continually being perfected but having as yet not achieved perfection. On our journey towards perfection we may slip, even fall at times, but if we continually get back up, shake off the dust, and return to the foot of the cross in repentance, the enemy will never have the upper hand.

There are two kinds of Christians, immature and mature. There are babes in the faith, and those who have matured and grown in their faith. All must pass through the babe stage, the infancy stage, but if we remain in that stage, if we continually find ourselves in the first grade, perched upon the first rung, we inevitably become spiritual brutes. We must heed the warning and the call to shake off the slumber, to repent of dead works, to come out of the spiritual infancy that so entices us, and press on toward the perfection that Christ came to reveal to all who have eyes to see and ears to hear. We must leave behind the elementary principles, and aspire to greater and deeper things in God.

The normal and natural life in Christ is a constant ascent toward perfection, a more intimate knowledge, a more complete obedience, and a more accurate similarity with Him. Where there is no growth there is no true spiritual health.

God's desire is to see all of His children become spiritually mature individuals, men and women who are able to rightly discern and rightly defend truth. God desires to see us becoming all that He promised we would be in Christ. He does not ask for much in order that He may give us much. Knowing all that we have access to in Christ by the power of the Holy Spirit, it would be foolish of us to be content with the lesser things. Why settle for the lesser when the greater things are within reach?

In Christ we have the perfect example and role model of what it is to achieve perfection: **A total submission to the Father's will, a complete obedience of His voice.** Christ is not only our example He is also the life and the power within us. Only by Him and in Him are we able to achieve perfection, which is none other than Christ made manifest in every area of our lives in uninterrupted continuity.

Only by growing and maturing in God are we able to overcome, to live a life of victory and not defeat, and to stand when others are fleeing. When one remains in a state of spiritual infancy and is unable to perform the duties required of them God has no choice but to replace them with another who has grown, is battle-ready, and is able to carry out His orders.

> Matthew 20:16, "So the last shall be first, and the first last. For many are called, but few are chosen."

Though many are called, only those who grow in God are chosen for greater things. Only the mature in God – those who are full of age and are able to consume solid foods – are entrusted with greater responsibility.

Hearing a teaching is one thing; living that teaching is another thing entirely. Just as the theory of light is different than light itself, so is hearing teaching on the will and order of God different from living them. We need teaching until we come to that point in our journey wherein we know it and have perceived its mysteries.

Then all that remains to be done is live the knowledge we have gleaned with conviction and boldness.

The principle objective of any teaching having to do with the divine, the supernatural, or spirituality is to lead us to life and birth within us a desire for the deeper things of God. It is when teaching births these desires in us that we know we have assimilated the message, having gone beyond the letter. If the teachings of Christ do not lead us to be more like Him, if they do not stir His Spirit in us, then we are not His.

True children of God go beyond the theoretical components of the Gospel and teachings of Christ, and they allow both the Gospel and Christ's teachings to mold them, to change them on the most basic of levels, to birth within them new desires, new goals, new aspirations, all of which are centered on the Kingdom of God, on the wisdom of God, and on the power of God. When I hear men speak of the things of this earth with such passion, when I hear them encourage their flocks to pursue material things, when their primary focus is on the now rather than on eternity, I realize with great sadness that they are still of this flesh, still of this world, shackled by the whims and desires of this present existence.

Romans 8:9, "But you are not in the flesh, but in the Spirit, if indeed the Spirit of God dwells in you. Now if anyone does not have the Spirit of Christ, he is not His."

What does this have to do with spiritual maturity one might ask? The answer, quite simply is, everything. A spiritually mature individual knows how to assign appropriate value to spiritual things as well as material things. A spiritually mature individual has realized the worthlessness of this present earth of material possessions, of fame and accolades, and pursues the true treasure, the priceless gifts, the spiritual insights that God gives only to those in whom He sees His Son. Though they may attend service regularly, and some may even be in leadership, the spiritually immature soul will always focus on this present life more than the eternal. They will always desire to make the flesh comfortable and at ease rather than build up their spiritual man.

Sovereign teaching, Godly wisdom, spiritual knowledge, all these serve to transcend the soul beyond the letter, beyond the symbolisms, beyond the traditions, beyond the formalities that are so pervasive in the church today, bringing them into the temple of the real, and into the kingdom of truth. Those who have passed beyond the confines of ceremony, of tradition, those who see the spirit beyond the letter, who live in complete surrender and constant expectation of the greater things of God, know true liberty, and true freedom. Intimacy with Christ allows us to rejoice in His constant presence and rest in God no matter the circumstances surrounding us.

One does not teach the doctrine of baptism to those who have already been baptized. It must be taught to those who have not yet been baptized. The constant rehashing of the elementary principles of Christ becomes almost painful to watch because these principles are being taught not to babes, not to those who have no experience in the Word, but those who have for years warmed a pew and sung in the choir. With each new generation of silver tongued, perfectly quaffed, impeccably dressed televangelists the same piece of earth is plowed over and over again, the same teachings are regurgitated, each one putting their own minor spin on it. Even so, if these teachings had anything even remotely to do with the will of God and the Word of God, I could overlook the constant repetition.

Sadly, God has been removed from the equation and Christ is rarely mentioned, yet those who trust the man behind the pulpit for their spiritual succor know no better because they are still babes, gratefully lapping up whatever is offered them since they do not have either the strength or the desire to go out and forage for themselves, to find sustenance on their own, and feed their starving spirits.

I am a firm believer in the idea that the Word of God and the will of God are simple enough for any man to understand. If one possesses a sincere heart unhindered by the blinders of denomination of preconceived notions, wisdom and knowledge of the divine are readily accessible.

For the rebellious, the cunning, and those who choose to hold on to unbiblical teaching, the truth of God's word will always be an unwelcome guest in their heart, and if the truth happens to make its way beyond the barriers they've put up they attempt to twist it so it fits agenda and ideology.

> 2 Corinthians 2:17, "For we are not, as so many, peddling the word of God; but as of sincerity, but as from God, we speak in the sight of God in Christ."

A person with no hidden agenda will tell you the truth even if the truth is painful to hear. It is love that compels the true servants of God to speak truth just as it is love that compels a parent to discipline a child when that child has disobeyed. A spiritually mature individual will realize that the truth was spoken in love even though the truth may be a rebuke. On the other hand, a spiritually immature individual will react as most children often react when they are rebuked, and even though it may have been done in love, they grow angry at being corrected and run into the embrace of the first peddler they come across, those unscrupulous souls who adulterate the Word of God for gain.

Because the babes – the immature souls among us – are unwilling to take correction, the synagogues of the peddlers are overflowing, and those who speak sincerely in the sight of God upholding the standard of truth, are mocked and ridiculed.

From a worldly standpoint compromise is the way to go. Spare the rod, spare the babes the truth that they need to repent and live up to God's standard, and you will have more success than you can handle. The problem is that you can't go to war with babes. One cannot lead an army of toddlers and babes onto a battlefield and expect victory. You go to war with warriors. You go to war with soldiers. You go to war with those who have proven themselves, who know the weapons of their warfare, and who will not retreat nor surrender in the face of opposition.

When seasoned warriors are taken into battle – men and women who have spent more hours on their knees than in front of the television, and men and women who trust in the strength of He who goes before them – victory is already a foregone conclusion. The question is no longer whether or not we will be victorious or whether or not we will overcome, but when?

The benefits of spiritual maturity are too many to number but one thing is certain: spiritual maturity is necessary for every believer. May we aspire and desire to grow in God, may we be full of age and consume the solid food of God's Word, journeying ever onward toward perfection, toward maturity, and toward being warriors useful to the Kingdom of God.

What's certain is that an immature Christian can never be a battle-ready believer. They are, by all accounts, useless in the battle with the enemy, for they are dependent upon others for their succor, and sustenance.

If we are mature enough, we understand our place in the Kingdom of God, as well as the Body of Christ. We understand our benefits, as well as our duty, we understand our advantages as well as our responsibilities, and as mature believers we do not shrink from, nor shy away from, them.

CHAPTER FIVE

HAVE YOU BUILT UP YOUR ENDURANCE?

Pretty much any fully grown adult can swing a sword once or twice. They can raise their shield to block the first blow, perhaps even the second, but without the requisite practice, without the requisite exertion, without the requisite endurance, they will be felled by the enemy sooner rather than later.

Yes, anyone can swing a sword a handful of times, even the most out of shape individual. However, only a handful of men have the endurance to be the last one standing in any given battle, to continue swinging and parrying and pivoting and guarding and deflecting and lunging until the last enemy is felled. Once you have learned how to fight, how to do battle, have done so from someone worth learning from, and have spiritually matured to the point of being equipped, the next step is to build up your endurance. It is not something that will happen overnight, and it cannot be hurried no matter how much we would like it to be so.

Ask any professional athlete what the secret to their success is, and you will invariable get a generic answer that comprises of two major themes: practice and endurance. Since we've already covered the practice aspect of our spiritual walk and battle-readiness in the previous chapter – exercising the sense by reason of use – I would now like to focus on the topic of building spiritual endurance. Just as physical endurance must be built up over time, spiritual endurance is a process. Even the healthiest, sedentary individuals cannot hope to keep pace over a ten mile run with someone who has been doing it for years or even months. The person who's never jogged a day in their life may be able to keep up the first few hundred yards, even the first mile, but eventually their lungs will start burning, their legs will grow weak, because he does not have the necessary endurance for prolonged activity.

Spiritual endurance is one of those topics that is rarely discussed but is of great importance. Everyone can put on the armor of God, helmet, breastplate, sword, shield, but only those with spiritual endurance are able to keep it on for prolonged periods of time. The reason spiritual endurance is necessary is a simple one: We do not choose the hour of our battle, we do not choose the season of our confrontation, but we are commanded of God to always be ready, to always be watchful, to always be prepared for that eventual and inevitable moment when the enemy will commence his onslaught.

There is no greater danger for a seasoned warrior, a mature servant of God, than to be caught off guard. It would be a dire predicament indeed if while the enemy is charging us, we are scrambling to find our armor, to put on our breastplate and our helmet, and unsheathe our sword.

A true warrior whose senses have been sharpened by battle is always prepared, always ready for the next confrontation, never letting down his guard, ever watchful. The enemy's tactics are well known. They have been documented throughout the scripture, and his propensity for surprise attacks is no secret. He waits patiently hoping that the soldiers of Christ will grow weary, he waits patiently hoping their endurance will run out, he waits patiently hoping they will lay down their swords and their shields – perhaps even rest their eyes for a while – and that is when he strikes.

We must also take into account that the enemy we face takes no prisoners. There is no Geneva Convention where prisoners of war must be treated with a modicum of humanity. There is no treaty written or implied wherein prisoners must be fed and housed appropriately. We cannot go into battle halfheartedly, hoping that even if we get taken prisoner a warm cot and some hot food will be waiting for us. We cannot take the battle lightly, believing that when it's all over we will be released, allowed to go back to our homeland wherein we will receive a hero's welcome. Again, the mortal enemy of our souls takes no prisoners. There are no cots to be had. There is no warm food to be eaten…just summary executions.

Those who came before us, the warriors who knew what it was to build spiritual endurance by prayer and fasting, watch in silence as this present generation must contend with enemies not only from without, but also from within. It is easy to defend oneself when the enemy is evident, clear, and well defined. It is much harder when you not only have to contend with the slings and arrows of the enemy from without, but also keep vigilant for the spiritual offspring of Judas and Brutus.

It is often that the traitors in our midst do more damage to the body of Christ than any attack of the enemy ever could. These are men without allegiance, men without conviction, men absent of loyalty who would readily betray those closest to them to advance their own agendas. The true servant of God, one who has built up spiritual endurance, learns to contend with such disappointments, keeping his eyes firmly planted on Christ and the cross, undaunted and undeterred. His purpose is clear: to overcome that he may inherit! Though trials may come, the soldier knows to trust the One who leads them into battle.

Hebrews 12:1, "Therefore we also, since we are surrounded by so great a cloud of witnesses let us lay aside every weight, and the sin which so easily ensnares us, and let us run with endurance the race that is set before us."

I wanted to begin the writing on spiritual endurance with this particular verse because it is so rich in wisdom. It is a wisdom that transcends time, language, and nationality. It is a verse overflowing with ever-relevant wisdom, and this above all else should lead us to conclude that it is a divine wisdom. Nothing in this world has the power of continuity like the Word of God does. It remains as important and necessary today as it was the day it was penned. There are three avenues that I would like to pursue in regards to this verse, three principles or ideas that should lead us to greater understanding concerning steadfastness in God, and building up spiritual endurance that we might not grow weary in battle.

The first truth gleaned from this verse is that as believers we are not alone. Although we may feel like it at times, although we might feel isolated and all by ourselves, a great cloud of witnesses surrounds us.

The second topic worthy of discussion is the laying aside of every weight, and the sin that so easily ensnares us. At this juncture one might ask what laying aside very weight could possibly have to do with spiritual endurance, and I'll just say that the less weight you carry on your back, the further you'll be able to march.

For now, we will leave it at that, but the implications of not being bogged down with the things of this world are wide ranging. If you are carrying extra weight you are automatically more sluggish. If you are more sluggish, you are an easier target. If your unit happens to be marching at a faster pace than you can manage with all the added weight, you will also fall behind and be an isolated target. Within the pages of Scripture, the devil is likened to a lion roaming about. This may not seem like any earth shattering revelation until you begin to understand the predatory instincts of a lion, as well as the fact that it is an apex predator. The natural instinct of any predator is to attack the weakest, most isolated, most defenseless animal in any given group. The predator is not looking for a fair fight, an honest fight, or a fight it believes it can be bested in. It is looking for prey. It is looking to devour. It is looking to destroy, and the easier the kill the better, because it translates to less expended energy on its part.

The third truth worth fleshing out in this verse is the faithful running of the race that is set before us, with endurance. All three principles are interconnected, and properly studied and applied can lead us to greater understanding.

First a few words on the great cloud of witnesses. No matter how far along we have come in the faith, or how much knowledge and wisdom we have accumulated, we cannot dismiss the truth that as believers we live the fullness of our faith today due to the revelations imparted to the saints that came before us. Without them, without those who came before us, men and women who paved the road of faith upon which we walk, without the light of God revealed through them, it would be a far more difficult a task for us to live lives of spiritual fulfillment in Christ today. It is one thing to walk an already well-worn path, it's quite another to venture into uncharted territory and not only blaze a trail, but the right trail.

Those who came before were tireless in their labors. They labored spiritually on a scale we have difficulty grasping, and due to the spiritual knowledge and experience they amassed we can, if we choose to take their experiences into consideration, live lives free of false starts, dead ends, and spiritual impediments.

Now that they have gone to their reward, the responsibility falls on us to labor as they did, and enrich the divine treasury, so those who come after us might benefit from our knowledge, as we have benefited from the knowledge of those who came before us.

Love for Christ compels us to make our own contribution, small as it might be, and insignificant as some might perceive it to be. What matters is that we labor, that we are faithful in our calling, that we press on ever toward the prize, that we are faithful stewards of that with which we have been entrusted, adding wisdom upon wisdom, and knowledge upon knowledge.

This same principle is plainly seen even in the natural world, wherein this present life is possible only due to the lives of those that came before. Not to sound too philosophical, but everything is interconnected in some way, whether great or small. I know that I became the man I am, in large part due to the wisdom that was passed down by my parents and grandparents, and by seeing their example lived out in a practical manner.

The saints of God, those who make up that great cloud of witnesses are above philosophers and poets, scribes and musicians, wise men, and kings. The crown jewels of this earth are God's saints. What makes a saint one might ask? It is not supernatural powers or the performing of miracles as some religions tend to believe. What makes a saint in God's eyes is faith and obedience toward Him, pure and simple.

Yes, there are those who came before us who are worthy of respect, but no man is worthy of reverence. I have too often seen the innocent elevate mere mortals to the status of demigods, and when these men proved themselves to be men, the innocent crumbled, losing their faith in the process, because their sights were not set higher. Caution is a necessity. We must beware that for the love of the saints we do not miss out on seeing God.

The saints of old are witnesses for those of us in this present generation of what faith can accomplish, and of how far one can grow in God. Men are mere signposts showing us the way, but are by no means our destination. A true man or woman of God will always defer to Jesus. They will always put the focus on Him rather than themselves, and strive to lift high the name Jesus rather than their own ministries.

As those that came before us, we run the race faithfully toward the goal and the prize knowing that God will keep us, and that we can with boldness enter the Holiest by the blood of Jesus. Christ consecrated this way for us, and as we grow in wisdom and knowledge, as we graduate and become soldiers, we will understand that we can with a true heart and full assurance of faith, enter into the mysteries of God and experience the divine, as did the forerunners of the faith.

The presence of God surrounds us. He is ever present, but He will not come in unwelcome. He will not force himself into the life of any man. We must endeavor to open our hearts, to allow Him in, and let Him purify and cleanse us, purge us of the flesh that He may indwell in our hearts perpetually. We must submit ourselves to God, and obey His commands, for only then will we be able to grow, mature, and ascend in the faith.

As the verse continues, we are counseled, even commanded to lay aside every weight and the sin that so easily ensnares us. Not every weight is a sin, but every sin is a weight. God's command is clear, and beyond debate. We are to lay aside every weight that we may run the race faithfully. If in a race one man has nothing attached to him and another is burdened with a one hundred pound pack on his back, it is obvious that the man with no weight pressing down on him will finish the race quicker, and be less weary at its end. With such a weight pressing down, it is questionable whether the man carrying the pack will even be able to finish the race.

The wisdom this verse is attempting to impart to all who have ears to hear is that there are certain things we must do as those who profess to believe. There are certain actions we must undertake in order to reach that point of sanctification God desires us to reach. As those who have received Him and believe in Him, we have the right to become children of God, but this requires the overcoming of stumbling blocks, snares, and everything else in the enemy's arsenal which he uses to cause the children of God to stop running, to become static, to grow no further and thereby become stagnant in their development. There are countless underdeveloped Christians walking about today and they are the enemy's primary objective. These are souls who have not attained spiritual maturity, have only partial knowledge of the things of God, and have not learned the fullness of that which they have access to in Him.

> John 1:12, "But as many as received Him, to them He gave the right to become children of God, even to those who believe in His name: who were born, not of blood, nor of the will of the flesh, nor of the will of man, but of God."

Steadfastness, boldness and courage are required of every believer in order to overcome. Though trials come we press on, though hardships abound we press on, though the snares are abundant we press on, though stumbling blocks are erected on a daily basis we press on. There is only one direction that a child of God can go, and that is forward. We do not retreat. We do not surrender. We do not lay down our arms nor take off our armor. With faith guiding our steps, and the knowledge that our heavenly Father is with us, we overcome, we press on boldly toward the prize that is within reach.

One of the greatest setbacks in the lives of believers, a setback which oftentimes stops them from attaining sanctification and compromises their relationship with God, is sin. Nothing more readily ensnares a life than sin. Whether great or small, if the sin goes unchecked, if it is not plucked out of our hearts and repented of, it drains us of our spiritual strength and eventually leads to death.

I write the following with all due solemnity: Dear brother, dear sister, be watchful over your own heart. There is nothing more important in this life than guarding against sin, and doing our utmost to rid ourselves of every weight. A man once said that there is no such thing as a small sin for even the smallest of sins desires your destruction, your separation from truth, and your return to the darkness from which grace plucked you. Too readily we dismiss the notion that we serve an omniscient God, but though we might dismiss the notion it does nothing to negate the factuality of it. We serve God who sees all things and knows all things, and if every day we woke up with this knowledge fresh upon our hearts, it would keep us faithful to the narrow path which has been revealed to us in the Word.

The last precept in this verse also goes to the title of this chapter, namely having spiritual endurance during the race that is set before us. A runner can only run if his legs are free, healthy, and he is aptly trained for the race that is set before him. No matter how good the athlete might be, it would be impossible for him to run a race if his legs were bound, or ensnared, or if he was suffering some debilitating illness. It is the same when spiritually applied.

Although Lazarus was alive, he could not walk because his legs were bound. Then Jesus said, 'loose him, and let him go.' One cannot walk the path much less run the race, unless they are free, unfettered, and absent of burdens and weights pressing down upon them.

All who run the race have time for nothing else, for the goal is singular: to finish it, to complete it, and to obtain the prize. Those who run consecrate themselves wholly to one purpose; the purpose of giving their all, of running faithfully until the end, and of crossing the finish line.

Without exception, all who run the race go through a checklist of six major things they do before the race, during the race, and after the race.

1. Anyone running a race prepares for it beforehand, building up their endurance and working toward their desired goal.

2. Anyone running a race prepares mentally as well as physically. After a certain number of miles, it becomes more of a mental struggle than a physical one, and in any given marathon close to half the participants will hit the wall at one point or another. Hitting the wall is essentially where fatigue and diminished mental faculties intersect, and those who prepare for the eventuality of it beforehand are able to push past it.

3. Anyone running a race studies the path the race will take, understands the route, is aware of the climate, and prepares accordingly. Everything is taken into account from elevation, to terrain, to time of year; all so one can do all that is in their power to do, and to ensure they've afforded themselves every opportunity to win the race.

4. Once the race begins the runner does not look back, is unconcerned with where he has been, and is concerned only with the next step, and with the path that lies before him.

5. You run the race to win not to place. You give it your all until the moment you cross the finish line. No one lags just because they're in the lead, because they know that if they slack off it's only a matter of time before someone will catch up and overtake them.

6. You save the celebration for after you finish the race. Few things are more cringe-worthy than those videos

wherein some runner or cyclist started celebrating too soon, lost their balance, tumbled, and missed out on placing first because of it. Make sure you finished the race, and then celebrate.

A faithful runner of the race, one who runs it with endurance, does not stop in the middle to retrace his steps, to ponder where he has been, but presses ever onward. One of the greatest dangers, one that threatens the spiritual lives of believers is thinking that they can stop along the way, content with the first experiences, satisfied with the initial touch, and complete after their first encounter during their journey. It's like a soldier in training raising their shield in time to deflect a blow, then putting down his weapons and walking away, satisfied in the knowledge that he was able to deflect that one blow.

Always be growing! Always be climbing! Always be learning! Always be maturing! Always be sharpening your skills! Stagnation leads to negligence of one's spiritual man, and leaves you stunted, immature, defenseless, and impotent.

True godliness does not consist only of drawing close to God, or of entering the Holiest, but of remaining there, existing there, every day throughout one's life, perpetually renewed and regenerated by His presence and Spirit. True godliness does not constitute merely raising our hand, or promising that we will endeavor to a new life in Him, but walking the path, living the life, knowing the cost and being willing to pay the price in full. This is the essence of endurance during the race in which we have engaged. This is the essence of endurance during the battle into which we have been conscripted.

I remember watching the Olympics some years ago, and after winning the gold medal, an athlete was explaining to a reporter how hard he had trained and all the sacrifices he had made to make certain that he was at the top of his game, and that he was ready to do his best. This athlete left nothing to chance, because chance is a fickle thing. In order to run the race faithfully we must be as committed, if not more so, than that athlete was, ready to deny the self, to lay aside every weight, to have a decided spirit, to not look back, and to persevere and overcome any obstacle or setback, having our gaze firmly set upon the finish line, and the prize that awaits.

Since spiritual illness is as real and destructive as physical illness, we must do our utmost to ensure that we are spiritually healthy, that our foundation is true, and our purpose is clearly defined. Although the spiritually infirm may start the race along with everyone else, eventually they give up, they give in, unable to continue for their ailment is holding them back, and inhibiting them from being able to press on. Sin causes spiritual illness. It weakens our spiritual man, and causes us to collapse along the path. If one is willing to be healed, if one seeks to be whole again, all that is required is to gaze toward the heavens and repent, leave behind that which hindered our walk, and let God lead us ever forward.

> *Hebrews 12:2, "Looking unto Jesus, the author and finisher of our faith, who for the joy that was set before Him endured the cross, despising the shame, and has sat down at the right hand of the throne of God."*

There is no greater example of endurance than Christ. After being encouraged to glean wisdom from those that came before us, the examples of the past, the heroes of the faith, Paul ends his symphony with the greatest example of all, Christ. If you believe the path has become too difficult, that you are required to sacrifice too much of this present life, that you have grown weary of battle, look to Jesus the author and finisher of your faith, and realize that for the joy that was set before Him, He endured the cross. Looking to Jesus and what He did, never fails to humble the heart of man.

I consider Paul to be the greatest, most inspired, and most prolific writer in scripture. I have spent countless hours and days perusing what amounts to a miracle of God's grace, of reading words that seem to ignite a fire in every soul that reads them. I have often wondered what made Paul such a powerful writer, and have come to believe that the power and the beauty of his writings can be summed up in one name: *Jesus!* Paul mentions the name of Jesus over 200 times in his writings, showing us that Jesus is the heart and mind of Paul. It is the fire that burned in him continually, the selfsame fire that drew so many souls to salvation. Although widely overlooked by many who would rather seek out verses promising them wealth and fortune, this verse which we are presently dissecting and studying, is one of the high points, one of the peaks of Paul's writing.

The central theme, and most important nugget of wisdom we can readily glean from this verse, is plain to see for anyone willing to see it. All things are contained in Christ, whether it is the past, the present or the future. If we have learned to look unto Jesus, all the mysteries are unraveled, all our seemingly unsolvable problems are solved. He is the consummation and the completion of our faith, of our love, and our wisdom.

When we are encouraged to look to Jesus, it is not merely to throw a passing glance once in a while, or see Him from our peripheral vision if the chance arises, but to have our gaze firmly planted upon him at all times. When one's gaze is firmly planted, he is able to look to nothing else except the object of his scrutiny. Blessed is the soul who has learned to do this one thing. Blessed is the soul who has learned to gaze upon Christ and Christ alone, without distraction. One who has learned to look to Jesus in perpetuity is no longer in danger of being misled, of falling into sin, of being defeated in battle, or of being deceived by the wolves of the world, for Christ is always before him.

When we look to Jesus we are assured a life of victory, an existence that is fruitful, a walk that is certain, and a path that is straight and narrow. Looking to Jesus casts both fear and shame from our hearts when it comes to being witnesses for Him, for always having Him before us keeps us fresh and alive in Him.

There is much we can learn from looking to Jesus, and as we continue to gaze upon His countenance, our eyes become more open to that which He has done, and that which is incumbent upon us to do.

May we look to Jesus and weep, for it was we who placed the crown of thorns upon his head. It was we who broke his heart. It was on our behalf that He was made a curse. It was our sins that pressed down so heavily upon Him. It was mankind, yes you and I, that caused the most painful of wounds. It was our sins that made Him cry out.

May we look upon Jesus and trust in Him. He died not only for our sins, but also for our salvation. So great was His grace, that He gave His life so we might have life, so great was His power, that the salvation offered to us is complete. All He asks is that we surrender and submit ourselves in totality, that we lay our burdens at the foot of the cross, and say as the Roman soldier of ages past, "truly this is the Son of God."

May we look upon Jesus and follow Him. He suffered of His own free will, compelled by love. We too must travel a thorny path, we too must put on our armor, we too must stand when others have fallen, we too must carry our crosses, but as Christ did, may we likewise prove our steadfastness, our faithfulness and endurance, as a good soldier should.

We must not grow weary, we must not give up, and we must press ever onward. We must confront persecution with a love fueled by courage, and endure the hardships with our hearts and minds firmly planted upon our Lord and Savior Jesus Christ.

Hebrews 2:10-11, "For it was fitting for Him, for whom are all things and by whom are all things, in bringing many sons to glory to make the author of their salvation perfect through sufferings. For both He who sanctifies and those who are being sanctified are all of one, for which reason He is not ashamed to call them brethren."

Throughout our journey on this earth we must never forget that Christ is the author of our faith. He is the One who has shown us the path we must walk, and the road we must follow. He guides us on the path of faith, a path He himself walked, a path He made possible for us. It is a path to which He calls all who would hear. Jesus Christ is the guide who shows us the way by which we may enter eternity.

Christ showed the world what faith could accomplish and what faith is. He showed the world its priceless worth, and how faith puts God above all else. He completes the work of faith in us when He becomes the object of our faith through the fact that He can transform us into His image and sanctify us unto Himself.

Christ's path on this earth was a path of suffering until the end. It was a marathon of suffering until the cross, and He endured to the end. He is the author of our faith only if we choose to walk the path that He has shown us. By His self-denial, obedience, and His very death He has shown us that there is no other way to God but the way of sacrifice, resisting both the world and our own flesh until the end. There is no other way to escape our fallen nature than to die to self.

We also rediscover what many of us have long known, that Christ is also the finisher of our faith. He is on the throne, and so makes this possible. Looking to Him, in His glory, we see the sure reward that awaits us if we persevere and overcome.

May we run the race, perpetually looking to our Lord Jesus. Not to ourselves, or our faith – be it weak or strong – but to the One whose very presence gives life to our faith. May we not look to ourselves, to our shortcomings and sins, but to the One who wiped away our sins, washed us in His blood, gave us new garments, and entrusted us with the Holy Spirit.

May we not look to the world and its temptations, but to He who said, **"I have overcome the world!"** May we not look to the enemy and his threats, but to the One who took away the enemy's power; to He who defends us and stands with us. May we not look to men for their approval or care for their opinion, but to Jesus our Emanuel the God who is with us, our King. If you need more faith, more endurance, more boldness, more steadfastness, more peace, more joy, look to Jesus, for the mystery of the Christian walk is revealed to us only in intimate fellowship with Him.

Hebrews 12:3, "For consider Him who endured such hostility from sinners against Himself, lest you become weary and discouraged in your souls."

As Paul continues his magnificent writing, he broadens upon the initial statement of looking to Jesus, and urges us to consider Him. Too often, whether it is a spiritual matter, or the Word, we have a tendency to gloss over them without giving them the necessary consideration, without pondering and contemplating, without learning the lesson that was right before our eyes. We are to look to Jesus, but also consider Him. Ponder and reflect upon His life, His lessons, and His actions.

No matter how great the pain might be, or how sharp the arrow of trial that has pierced you, no matter how hurtful the rejection of those around you, nothing can compare with the sufferings of our beloved Savior. Trials are difficult and become unbearable when we dwell on the trial itself, on our own circumstance, and not on Christ. May we all the more look to and consider Christ in the midst of our trials, the selfsame Christ who was made perfect through sufferings. May we consider the Man of sorrow, and we will receive the comfort of His mercy, the courage of His character, and the joy of being likened unto Him in our sufferings.

There is a reason we must consider Christ and the hostility He endured from sinners against Himself, and it is so we do not become weary and discouraged in our souls. Weariness and discouragement are first birthed in the soul of a man, and then become visible on his outer countenance. If our souls are at peace and rested in Christ, even if the body undergoes strenuous labors, it is kept strong.

When one loses heart he is no longer able to do much good. I have witnessed many a soul who have lost heart, who go from one defeat to another, from one loss to another, growing all the more discouraged and despondent. There is a sure way by which we will not lose heart, and that is to give our hearts to Christ, and sanctify the Lord God in them.

The heart in which Christ resides cannot be overcome by adversity or sin. Such a heart is no longer subject to the flesh, no longer at the whim of dead influences, but alive in the One who redeemed it. Look to Christ and consider Him, and you will have ample endurance, ample faith, ample boldness to run the race faithfully and joyfully, knowing that when your race is complete, the crown of life awaits you as reward for your steadfastness.

CHAPTER SIX

DO YOU UNDERSTAND YOUR AUTHORITY?

You've got to give credit where credit is due. The devil is very, very good at marketing. Only someone who is brilliant at marketing can compel certain individuals to believe hell is a nice place, heaven is passé, the devil is good, God is unloving, and Christians have no authority to speak of.

The only ones to come close to the audacity of the devil in our modern era are the tobacco industry, wherein they tell you their product will literally kill you on their packaging, and still expect you to go out and pay for the privilege of committing slow suicide. And yet, here they are a multi-billion-dollar industry with an unending slew of new customers to replace the ones who are dying for having used their product.

You can sell pretty much anything if you just pitch it right, and it seems the enemy is pitching eternal darkness in such a manner wherein less and less individuals are concerned about ending up there, and more and more people are actually enthused by the prospect.

You've all heard the foolish quips like *'better to reign in hell than serve in heaven,'* but who exactly told you, you were going to reign in hell? Who said hell was anything other than eternal flame and the gnashing of teeth, that place where the worm never dies?

It was the enemy and he's done a bang up job because he knows how to market. They've even produced television shows depicting Lucifer as a soft touch sort of fellow who is largely misunderstood, and who just wants to let his hair down and have a little fun once in a while. It's in the marketing that hell is portrayed as an attractive place and the devil as playful farceur. So you've got a bunch of young people who are excited about the prospect of hell, who consider themselves full blown Satanists, because the marketing was so overwhelming for them.

We all know the reality of what hell is by what Jesus told us it was. We know it is not a place anyone will ever want to go to voluntarily, yet here we are, and fools are lining up for the opportunity.

The same can be said for sin, which is ultimately destructive, which ultimately causes men and women alike to destroy their own lives for a momentary, fleeting pleasure that they forget about as soon as the consequences of their sin comes to bear.

If you've seen commercials on television, or heard them on the radio, you know there is such a thing as positive marketing, and negative marketing. Especially when it comes to politicians and election season, you hear a lot of negative marketing regarding their competition. If someone is running against them, you hear how the other guy is dishonest, and a charlatan, how if he's elected things will go from bad to worse. Likewise, the enemy uses positive as well as negative marketing when it comes to himself and the children of God.

Not only is sin promoted, glorified, made to look less like the destructive force it is and more like something to revel in, but the children of God are made to look as weak, rudderless individuals who have little more than their churches and the hymns they sing every Sunday morning.

We are portrayed as the outcasts, behind with the times, hopelessly stuck in our ways, and unwilling to embrace progress for all that it is. We are portrayed as enemies of logic, enemies of intellect, enemies of reason, and made to seem as though what we believe is on equal footing as those who believe in unicorns, or think themselves wizards from a magical land in another dimension.

The household of faith has been berated, maligned, denigrated, besmirched, ostracized, and even taken to task by those whom many look up to as their spiritual leaders, for not towing the line and no longer calling sin, sin, or darkness, darkness.

Yes, hatred, vitriol, even persecution are expected from those of the world, but the sad and tragic thing is that even those within the church are being swayed and influenced to distance themselves from those who practice righteousness and hunger after holiness, and they do it vociferously for fear of being clumped in with the zealots and fundamentalists.

We are willing to betray truth, we are willing to betray righteousness, we are willing to betray God Himself just to make nice with the enemy and be accepted by his minions.

Isaiah 5:20, "Woe to those who call evil good, and good evil; who put darkness for light, and light for darkness; who put bitter for sweet, and sweet for bitter."

We read this verse and many like it, we understand what it says, what it means, and why the warning is so dire, and then we give heed to the voices that somehow convince us it's not talking about them. We allow ourselves to be convinced that these verses are not talking about those sowing deception in the house of God, that they're not even talking about the people of God, and that they're talking about someone else, some other people, and some other group of folks.

The truth, the hard truth, the cold truth, is that these who would call evil good, and good evil that Isaiah speaks of are found within the house of God, among God's people, and many of them hold positions of power within the organized church system, and within certain denominations.

The same chapter in Isaiah that warns against those who would call evil good, and good evil, reveals this truth to us just a few verses later.

> *Isaiah 5:25-26, "Therefore the anger of the Lord is aroused against His people; He has stretched out His hand against them and stricken them, and the hills tremble. Their carcasses were as refuse in the midst of the streets. For all His anger is not turned away, but His hand is stretched out still."*

Who is the anger of the Lord aroused against? Yep, it's right there, in black and white: *"the anger of the Lord is aroused against His people!"*

Not against those of the world, not against those who are ignorant of the power and authority they possess in God, but against His people, those who ought to know better, and still wallow in self-defeat, still wallow in doubt, still wallow in this spiritually suicidal duplicity that has become the norm in so many churches and for so many believers.

The anger of the Lord is aroused against His people, because He holds His people to a higher standard.

The anger of the Lord is aroused against His people, because they ought to know better than to fall for the lies of the enemy. As children of God we should know the enemy's tactics, we should know how the enemy works, and have the presence of mind to counteract his actions and put an end to his plans.

Among the many negative marketing campaigns the enemy has aimed at the believer, one stands out to me as the most dangerous, the most destructive, and in certain circles the most successful. The campaign I am referring to centers around the premise that as believers we are powerless, we have no authority to speak of, and we are simply at the mercy of the enemy and his minions.

The success of this campaign hinged on man's unwillingness to exert himself in seeking the greater things of God, and man's proclivity to finding excuses for not pressing in, not growing in God, and not taking the fight to the enemy.

We've been on the defensive for so long as a church body, and as the army of God, that we don't know what it is to be on the offensive anymore. We don't know what it is to take the fight to the enemy, to see the enemy flee from before us, and to see the power of our God made manifest.

The reason for this, the reason we seem to cower every time we see the enemy approaching, the reason we seem to be fleeing from before the enemy, is because we've been lulled to sleep and convinced to believe the lie that as believers we have no power whatsoever, no weapons to speak of, and no means by which to do battle against the darkness.

You've got very famous preachers teaching this, you've got men who are respected across denominational lines spewing this nonsense, and the church is eating it up.

Why? It's simple! If we no longer have access to power, if we no longer have access to gifts, if we no longer have any authority, then the problem does not lie with us, or our duplicity, or our *lukewarmness,* or our divided hearts.

It's just not available, and that's why we don't have it! God simply discontinued this feature, and no matter how hard you go looking you're just not going to find it.

We've found the perfect excuse to be lukewarm. We've found the perfect excuse to be indifferent. We've found the perfect excuse to waste away the days doing absolutely nothing, because there really isn't anything we can do.

That whole authority thing, that whole power thing, that whole gifts thing, that ended with the disciples, so we can talk about their stories, and we can tell each other what God did through them, but God just can't do the same through us, because contrary to what Jesus said, there was a time limit on the Holy Spirit, and there was a time limit on the gifts of the Holy Spirit.

Do you realize how utterly pathetic that would be? Do you realize how hopeless and absent of any glimmer of optimism that would sound?

"Well, you have an enemy, he really hates you, so much so that he's been compared to a roaring lion seeking whom he may devour, but there's nothing you can do about it. If he gets your scent, if you cross his path, if you somehow manage to draw his attention, then you're done for. You can't outrun a lion, and since you don't have any weapons, you're no match for him, so it's just better to keep your head down, not make any waves, keep quiet, and go along."

That's pretty much the message from the mouths of most preachers today! Keep your head down, keep quiet, don't make waves, and go along!

But is that what Jesus said? Did Jesus say we would be weaponless and powerless and absent authority? Did He say that the only time period we could hope to overcome, conquer, and beat back the enemy was while the apostles were still alive?

If that's what He said, then I guess that's how it is, and I would be a very sad, very desolate, very fearful soul.

So, what did Jesus say?

Luke 10:19-20, "Behold, I give you the authority to trample on serpents, and scorpions, and over all the power of the enemy, and nothing shall by any means hurt you. Nevertheless do not rejoice in this, that the spirits are subject to you, but rather rejoice because your names are written in heaven."

So Jesus is speaking to seventy men who had just gone out in His name, and had seen the power of God manifest through them. The sick were healed, demons were cast out, and they realized that even the demons were subject to them in Christ's name.

They had gone out with no money bag, no sack, no sandals, pretty much broke and barefoot and even antisocial since they were told not to greet anyone along the way, and returned full of joy because they had seen the authority they had in Christ's name manifest through them firsthand.

Once you see the power of God working in you and through you, once you understand what it is to walk in the authority of Christ, then the material things, the earthly things, whether or not you have a money bag, or even sandals, will become irrelevant.

So knowing that Christ gave us His authority, it would be wise, and even prudent to understand what authority truly means, and what it means to walk in the authority of Christ.

The word **authority** can be defined as power, charge, supremacy, jurisdiction or command.

When we speak of someone having authority, it is usually something that was entrusted to an individual, and though in and of themselves the individuals might be powerless, because they have the authority of the office, or the authority of a certain institution behind them, they demand obedience, or adherence.

A politician has authority because the people elected him to the office, and the office gives him the aforementioned authority.

A policeman has authority because society has granted him said authority.

Why does this notion of authority matter?

Well, let's say a guy in board shorts tries to stop you in the middle of the road. Would you give him a second thought? Would you even entertain the idea of stopping just because he held out his hand, or would you think him a bit soft in the head?

Now we take that selfsame individual, put him in a police uniform, and when he extends his hand, because of the authority we associate with the badge and the uniform, we stop our vehicle even though it's still the same person. Because of the authority we perceive the individual possesses, we stop even though it's the same guy.

Christ has given us authority. This means that when we command the enemy in Christ's name, it's not Mike that he sees or hears. It's not Mike that he fears, but the authority of Christ which Mike possesses.

This is why the enemy is so hell-bent on keeping the believer blind to his authority in Christ, because he knows the difference the authority of Christ makes in the life of the believer.

Absent the authority of Christ, my commanding the devil would be like the guy in the board shorts trying to direct traffic. People would look, shake their heads, but not really do what the individual in the board shorts asks of them.

If, however, I am clothed in Christ and I have the authority of Christ, then I'm not the guy in the board shorts anymore, I'm the guy in the uniform, with the badge, empowered by the office, and having authority!

So the first question we must ask ourselves – and it is a painful one because it requires inward introspection – is are we in our uniform, walking in the authority of our General, or are we wearing board shorts trying to tell the devil what to do while he's laughing at us?

Rather than understand the true and full meaning of authority in Christ and what it is to have authority to trample on serpents and scorpions and the power of the enemy, some have taken to physically attempting to prove their authority by handling live snakes or scorpions.

To those individuals I would simply say that they've missed the boat entirely, and have disregarded the Word of God when it comes to the battle we fight, and who it is we are fighting it against.

2 Corinthians 10:3-6, "For though we walk in the flesh, we do not war according to the flesh. For the weapons of our warfare are not carnal but mighty in God for pulling down strongholds, casting down arguments and every high thing that exalts itself against the knowledge of God, bringing every thought into captivity to the obedience of Christ, and being ready to punish all disobedience when your obedience is fulfilled."

But what about proving our authority by handling poisonous snakes?

It's not what Jesus was referring to, and we ought to know that by now. Though we walk in the flesh, we do not war according to the flesh. My handling of a snake or a scorpion will do nothing to hurt the enemy, or cause him to retreat. Me walking in the authority of Christ and rebuking the enemy and pulling down strongholds and casting down arguments and bringing every thought into captivity to the obedience of Christ, that, my friends, will hurt the enemy, it will cause him to flee, for in our resisting the devil he flees from us.

James 4:7, "Therefore submit to God. Resist the devil and he will flee from you."

There you go. Simple as pie! First, submit to God, then, resist the devil and he will flee from you. The issue at hand, however, is that most believers today haven't even done the first part, never mind the second part.

They've not submitted to God, not in reality, and if one has not submitted to God then they neither have the authority of Christ nor the power to resist the devil.

What we must remember is that the seventy who returned to Christ with joy, amazed at the fact that even demons were subject to them in His name, were already disciples of Christ. They weren't just some guys Jesus found on the street corner, they were not some uninitiated men who thought it would be fun to forfeit everything in their present life so they can go from town to town getting rejected.

These were already disciples. These men already knew Jesus, they already believed in Jesus, they already desired to be like Jesus, they had already committed to following after Jesus, and only then were they sent out into the towns to preach.

The first prerequisite to walking in the authority of Christ is to know Christ. It is to believe in Jesus, not as some mystical figure, not as a prophet, not as a good guy with some nice life lessons, but as the Son of the living God. As He who was born of a virgin, died on a cross, and rose again on the third day as just recompense for you and me. Believe in Jesus!

Believe in the Jesus of the Bible, not some variation thereof made palatable by the world and those whose desire is not to serve, or submit, or humble themselves, but live the life they want to live and have some sort of fire insurance along the way.

John 14:12-17, "Most assuredly, I say to you, he who believes in Me, the works that I do he will do also; and greater works than these he will do, because I go to My Father. And whatever you ask in My name, that I will do, that the Father may be glorified in the Son. If you ask anything in My name, I will do it. If you love me, keep My commandments. And I will pray the Father and He will give you another Helper, that He may abide with you forever, even the Spirit of truth, whom the world cannot receive, because it neither sees Him nor knows Him; but you know Him, for He dwells with you and will be in you."

So let's break this down a little bit. You may think it is off topic, but it's not. The Holy Spirit, the Helper as Jesus calls Him is the One who is with us today, who abides with us, and who empowers us to walk in the authority of Christ.

Jesus gave us the authority; the Holy Spirit empowers us to walk in it.

So Jesus begins by delineating who it is that will be able to do greater works than what He did, by saying "he who believes in Me!"

It's not just anyone. It's exclusive. It's reserved. It is only those who believe in Him!

Then Jesus proceeds to tell us that He will do whatever we ask in His name, that the Father may be glorified in the Son. "If you ask anything in My name I will do it." These were the words of Jesus.

So I was preaching this passage in a church one time and after the service a lady came up to me and said, I've been asking to win the lotto for thirty years and it hasn't happened. So what happened to that *"If you ask anything in My name."*

She seemed like a sincere enough lady, but sincerity is no excuse for ignorance. As such, I sat down with her and explained that there are keys to this promise, the first being *"he who believes in Me!"* the second being *"that the Father may be glorified in the Son."*

If I truly believe in Christ, then my mind is no longer on the things of this earth, my desires are no longer tethered to the material, and when I ask Him for something, it will not be something as wasteful as material possessions.

Would God be glorified in her winning the lotto? Would God be glorified in her having an excess of material possessions? Would someone whose reason for being was to serve Jesus even ask such a thing?

If you believe in Jesus, then your focus is already shifted from the things of this earth to the things above. If you believe in Jesus, your hope already rests in the life to come and not this present life. If you believe in Jesus then all you ask of Him, at its root, will be to glorify God, and not to appease the flesh.

He who believes will live as though he believes, and ask as though he believes!

Jesus continues and adds another component, and that is love.

"If you love me, keep my commandments."

So first believe, and then love Him. Now if you love Him, truly love Him then Jesus says it must be an active love. *If you love Me, keep My commandments.* If you truly love Him, then that love will motivate you, it will compel you, it will drive you to keep His commandments.

If you love Him, that love will not allow you to be indifferent, it will not allow you to be lukewarm, and it will not allow you to be lethargic. It will drive you to a greater knowledge of Him, and compel you to spiritual maturity in Christ.

Just as a test of logic, if loving Jesus means keeping His commandments, what does not loving Jesus look like?

Would it be a reasonable thing to assume that if you love Him it means you keep His commandments, and if you don't love Him it means you don't?

Love is more than just words coming out of our mouths. If I tell my wife I love her but never pay her any mind, am not attentive, am not affectionate, do not take her opinions into consideration, step out on her every chance I get, then blame her for every wrong thing in my life, does that really mean I love my wife?

Many people today claim to love God, but their actions say otherwise. It's just the way it is. Sorry if I'm ruining someone's Tuesday night.

We say we love God with our lips but our hearts are given over to our idols, to the things we want to do, to things we want to pursue, the aspirations we cloister deep within our beings, that have nothing to do with Jesus, and are very often in direct and diametrical opposition to His commandments.

"And I will pray the Father and He will give you another Helper, that He may abide with you forever, even the Spirit of truth, whom the world cannot receive, because it neither sees Him nor knows Him; but you know Him, for He dwells with you and will be in you."

Since this is not a chapter on the Holy Spirit, I just want to point out one more thing before we return to the authority of the believer, and that is something Jesus said in regards to the Holy Spirit's continuity, or presence with those who believe, and love Him. *"I will pray the Father and He will give you another Helper, that He may abide with you forever."*

Words of Jesus! Indisputable! Undeniable! Words of Jesus!

But see, the enemy knowing that the Holy Spirit would abide with the believer forever, and that by way of the Holy Spirit we would be able to walk in the authority of Christ, he began an all-out campaign to do away with the notion of the person of the Holy Spirit, as well as the gifts, weapons, defenses, and authority His presence implies.

Gifts, what gifts? Power, what Power? Authority, what authority?

No, that was just for another time, in another place, for another people, we're just stuck with our pseudo-intellectual blowhards, pretend theologians, and evangelists full of hot air who insist they are the answer to your troubles rather than Jesus, and that power and authority are no longer available to any of us.

God has not left us powerless against the prince of this world. He has given us an arsenal of weapons, which we can use as believers, and the authority of Christ, which makes the enemy subject to us in Christ's name.

It is not me the enemy fears; it is Christ in me. It is not me the enemy flees from; it is the authority of Christ flowing through me that causes him to retreat.

I realize we're all excited about the prospect of having demons subject to us and being able to rebuke them and cast them out, but before we do anything of the sort we must first know with certainty that we are clothed in Christ.

In order to have the authority of Christ, we must be clothed in Christ. Otherwise, the enemy will run right over us, and even shame us in the process.

It would be a horrible, horrible thing to hear an evil spirit say, "Jesus I know, and Paul I know; but who are you?"

I don't know about you, but that would make my blood run cold. Hence the reason we must know that we believe, and love, and obey Him before we venture out to do things in His name.

If you have not a clue what I am referring to, well, I am referring to the seven sons of Sceva, who was himself a Jewish chief priest.

These seven young men grew up in a religious home, their father was a religious man, a chief priest in fact, and they decided among themselves this was close enough to the mark in order to cause an evil spirit to come out of a man.

They neither knew Christ or followed Him, they neither obeyed Him or served Him, yet these seven brothers convinced themselves into believing that if they spoke what they likely heard others speaking, then they too could boast about casting out a demon. Their only frame of reference was a sermon they'd heard Paul preach in which he spoke of Jesus.

So the seven sons of Sceva got together and found a man in whom an evil spirit resided and said, "We adjure you by the Jesus whom Paul preaches."

As I said, their only connection with Jesus was the fact that they'd heard Paul talking about Him. They did not know Him personally, they did not believe in Him, they did not love Him; they just knew it worked for Paul, so it should work for them as well.

Well, it didn't work for them, because although the evil spirit within the man knew of Jesus, and knew of Paul, he had no clue who these seven young men were.

Make sure Jesus knows you! The only way Jesus will know you, is if you know Jesus, and not from a secondary source, not through a surrogate, not through a third party, but firsthand: You and Him.

If Jesus knows you, I guarantee you the enemy knows you as well, and if the enemy knows you, and knows you walk in the authority of Christ, he is leery of you.

The enemy didn't know the seven sons of Sceva, because they'd never met Jesus, they were not clothed in Christ, and as such they did not walk in His authority.

So what happened? Did they part as friends? Did the evil spirit in the man say "better luck next time?" Did they play a round of cards, have some ice tea, and call it a day?

Acts 19:16, "Then the man in whom the evil spirit was leaped on them, overpowered them, and prevailed against them, so that they fled out of that house naked and wounded."

So we can see the glaring difference between the seventy disciples who Christ sent out, and who came back joyful, and the seven sons of Sceva who ran out of the house naked and wounded having been overpowered by a man in whom an evil spirit resided.

That's the difference between knowing Jesus, believing in Him, and loving Him enough to deny yourself, and having heard about Him from someone, having heard what He can do, and what He has done.

To walk in the authority of Christ is to know that He walks with you, and before you, and behind you, that you are shrouded in Him, clothed in His righteousness, and more than an overcomer through Him.

It's amazing to me how many believers are fearful about tomorrow, or what's happening in the government, or what is soon to happen, because we are given to know these things simply to prepare spiritually, not to be fearful of them.

If God foreknew, then He has already prepared a way for you and me as long as we truly believe, and not just say we do. I know that my God lives, I know that my God is able, I know that the just will live by faith, and if the day will come when the world strips me of everything, the one thing they will never be able to strip me of is Jesus, and He is enough.

> *Romans 8:35-39, "Who shall separate us from the love of Christ? Shall tribulation, or distress, or persecution, or famine, or nakedness, or peril, or sword? As it is written: 'For Your sake we are killed all day long; we are accounted as sheep for the slaughter.' Yet in all these things we are more than conquerors through Him who loved us. For I am persuaded that neither death nor life, nor angels nor principalities nor powers, nor things present nor things to come, nor height nor depth, nor any other created thing, shall be able to separate us from the love of God which is in Christ Jesus our Lord."*

Are these four verses real to you? Are these four verses a reality in your life? Is there anything you've allowed to get in the way of your relationship with Jesus? Is there anything you've allowed to keep you from walking in His authority? Is there anything you prize above Him? I know these are difficult questions, but they are necessary questions.

Paul didn't say that death or life or angels or principalities or powers or things present or things to come couldn't persuade him, he said he *wasn't* persuaded by them.

It is imperative we realize what Paul was trying to say. He didn't say I *cannot* be persuaded, he said, "I am not persuaded."

There is a marked difference there, and it all has to do with where Jesus is in your heart, and whether or not He has the place of honor there.

Your authority as a believer stems from your relationship with Jesus. If throughout this book you've latched on to any truth, let it be this one.

Your authority as a believer stems from your relationship with Jesus.

If your relationship with Jesus is nonexistent, then you have no authority to speak of. It's that simple. I can't sugarcoat it; I won't sugarcoat it!

If you only know of Christ but don't know Christ, then if I were you I wouldn't attempt to cast out demons or command principalities to flee, because you have no authority, you are the guy in the board shorts trying to direct traffic.

First obedience, first humility, first discipleship, first the knowledge of the Lordship of Christ, the Kingship of Christ, then, once you are clothed in Him, once you are clothed in His righteousness, you are walking in His authority.

Men of God do great exploits in His name because they know Him, and He knows them, not because they are special in and of themselves.

May we be humble enough to realize our power is not ours but His, our authority is not ours but His, and that we are not victorious in and of ourselves, but by Him and Him alone.

Once we lay hold of this reality, once we know that we have authority in Christ and through Christ, we will walk with boldness and do battle with the enemy fearlessly, all the while giving glory to God for the authority He has given us.

CHAPTER SEVEN

DO YOU KNOW YOUR WEAPONS?

Not everyone who claims to be a soldier is in fact a soldier. In a world wherein more and more people spend more and more time in virtual realities, removed and disconnected from life, it may be hard for some to understand that there are prerequisites to being a soldier that extend beyond calling yourself one.

There are three prerequisites to being a soldier and it goes beyond buying an outfit at the army surplus store.

1. Enlistment

2. Training

3. Equipment, Gear, or Arsenal

In order for someone to be a soldier in word and in deed, they must enlist, go through basic training, and be assigned the requisite gear for combat.

You can have the best training but if you don't have the gear you are prey.

You can have the best gear but if you don't know how to use it, you are prey.

You can have both training and gear, but if you are not enlisted, if you don't belong to a battalion, if there aren't others fighting alongside you and you are not taking orders from a commanding officer, you will not be long for this world.

A soldier without weapons is a soldier in name only, as is a soldier without proper training, or a chain of command. A soldier who is not proficient in the use of his weapons is a soldier at a disadvantage. Even though the movies insist that one man with a toothpick, a shoelace, and a compass can take on an entire army on foreign soil without knowing the terrain, between the guy with the knife and the guy with the gun, the guy with the gun usually wins.

If two men of equal proficiency only differed in the weapons at their disposal, then logic would dictate the man who was better equipped, and who had access to more weapons, would win out over the one who was not.

Meeting the enemy on the battlefield is a hard enough task when we are fully equipped, trained, and have every weapon at our disposal in our arsenal. Even then, the devil gets in a few blows. Even then the devil manages to fell some, and these are usually men who we considered invincible, and beyond the enemy's reach. This often happens if the individual in question is either distracted, or not sufficiently equipped for the task at hand.

As I've said before, the easiest way to get one's clock thoroughly cleaned is to underestimate one's enemy and go into battle unprepared, unfocused, and ill equipped.

We cannot take anything for granted in battle. No soldier ignores the fundamentals of making sure his gear is clean, and that everything is working as it ought, because he knows his life depends on whether his gun will fire, or his sword will cut.

We must make it a priority to not only make certain we have all the spiritual weapons we can get our hands on in our possession, we must also make certain they are ready for warfare when the time comes.

I have quite a few friends who are into guns, who own guns and enjoy shooting them at the range or to go hunting. To the last, every man is meticulous about cleaning his weapon after use, making sure everything is as it ought to be for the next time he goes out shooting or hunting.

This notion of always being ready, of always having sharpened swords and battle-ready armor must be as second nature to us. It must become an extension of who we are, and what we are.

A soldier never stops being a soldier, nor should a Christian ever stop being a Christian regardless of his surroundings, or the people he comes in contact with.

I see a man in uniform and I know what branch of the armed forces he serves in. I know whether he is Navy, Army, Marine, or Air Force based on the aforementioned uniform. Men should likewise be able to tell we are Christians by our countenance, our conduct, our speech, our decisions and our behavior.

No, it's not about works, it's about mirroring Jesus. It is not about earning our salvation, but rather about manifesting what the fruit salvation ought to have wrought in us upon encountering the Christ.

Words without action are meaningless. Once again using my wife as an example, I can tell her I love her, but if my every action contradicts my proclamation, she will realize something is amiss. She will see that all I am doing is saying some words which have no meaning, because there is no action undergirding them.

Many today say they love Jesus, then never do a thing to show that love. They have no desire to spend time with Him, they have no desire to serve Him, they have no desire to obey Him, they have no desire to know Him, and yet, they proclaim and vociferously so, that they belong to Him. Many today say they are soldiers for the cause of Christ, and never follow through in defending the selfsame Christ for whom they said they were a soldier.

It is because they follow through with action that some men are counted to be men of their word, and not simply because they spoke the words.

I know men who are men of their word, and I know blowhards who talk a big game but never follow through with anything. I know men who say little and do much, and I also know men who say much and do little.

It's not about the words; it's about the action. It's not about the theory of faith and salvation; it's the practical application of faith and salvation that we must endeavor to live out daily.

The same is true for those who consider themselves soldiers for Christ. There is a marked difference between a man who says and a man who does, and the man who does usually doesn't say so much. The man who does knows the hardships of battle, he knows the draining effects it has on one's vitality, and he knows there is no glory in war but only in victory. As such, he does all he can to stand victorious when the dust has settled and the departed have been counted.

There are a lot of talkers out there, but fewer and fewer doers. Most of the time people are too busy promoting themselves, their new books, their new products, their *magic water from the wellspring of the forgotten fountain,* or some other nonsense, to be bothered with actually doing something for the Kingdom. It is sad, but it is likewise true, and all one need to in order to see the veracity in my words is to open their eyes and look around.

People nowadays seem to have an aversion to doing. They have an aversion to getting their hands dirty, or exerting themselves, or risking anything more than a couple dollars each Sunday at church.

If we desire to be soldiers of the cross, if we desire to be warriors in the truest sense of the word, then every day, all day, without fail, we risk it all. We lay our lives on the line, we obey our orders without equivocation, and we go about the hard task of *doing* that which we were commanded to do, without attempting to second guess God, without attempting to question our orders, without trying to pass the buck and get someone else to do the heavy lifting in our stead. We do the work because have been called upon to do the work, and because we know that the God who sees all, will reward all in due season.

We need soldiers. We need laborers. We need men and women who are willing to roll up their sleeves and put in a hard day's work day after day. There is no need for idle management or people who enjoy talking about doing the work but never really getting around to it. Useless are those who wax poetic about warfare but never once dared to stand on a battlefield.

We need obedient servants. We need self-denying, selfless soldiers in our day and age more than ever before, because the darkness is growing, and is infringing upon the most sacred of places. All the while, the church seems to be lethargic at best or indifferent at worst. In a time when the alarms should be blaring, the church is asleep. In a time when the watchmen should be on the wall, they're out playing golf. In a time when the people of God ought to be wholly committed to the cause of Christ, duplicity and doublemindedness are all the rage among believers.

Look around for yourself, and if you don't think it's true or you believe I'm missing something let me know, because it is disheartening to see the church in the spiritual condition that it's in, especially since time is so short, and the end of all things is so close at hand.

Of all the things we've discussed throughout this book, one of the things we have yet to delve into is a warrior's weapons.

When it comes to weapons, there are weapons of defense, weapons of attack, and weapons that in a pinch can pull double duty and be used both for attack as well as for defense. The believer's arsenal of weapons is clearly itemized within God's Word, and this is done so we can go through the checklist, inventory our gear, see if anything is missing, and if we are, in fact, ready for battle.

Although the notion of preparedness has fallen out of favor in recent times, like so many other practical and necessary virtues, one understands the true importance of preparedness only when it's too late.

If I only realize my shield is rusty and my blade is when I take my stand on the battlefield, it is likely too late to do anything about it. If we do not do our utmost to prepare for the eventuality of battle, even before the battle begins the enemy has a distinct advantage due to our failure to assign the correct level of importance to the task of preparation, making sure our armor and our weapons are as they ought to be.

Nowadays Christians seem to be suffering defeat at the hands of the enemy more than at any other time in history not because the enemy has gotten better at what he does, but because the average believer has grown more slothful, more indifferent, and more concerned with the affairs of this life rather than the life to come.

The devil is still the devil, but the caliber of soldier has consistently decreased over the years to what is now a woeful, unacceptable level.

We play church, we play soldier, we play at being saved and at obeying God's Word, and then wonder to ourselves why defeat seems to be a constant, like an ever present shadow, never far and always in sight.

There was a time when believers were encouraged to spend time with God in prayer, when they were encouraged to read the Word of God and learn to hear His voice rather than buy the latest and greatest teaching series on how positivity can transform your life, or how you can spice up your love life the Christian way.

Incrementally but consistently we've made the Christian walk about ourselves rather than about servitude toward God, and every teaching seems to be focused on how we can better enjoy this present life and exploit God's love for us by continually demanding material excess.

It is a sad and tragic thing when an entire generation goes from knowing God on a personal and intimate level, to only knowing men who know God and speaking of them in hushed and reverent tones as though they were something more than mere men because they have a relationship with the Father.

It is in the fact that we see things such as prophecy, dreams, visions, revelation, gifts of healing, discernment, tongues or interpretation of tongues as special or rare that we can know just how off track the church has gotten, and how ill prepared we are when it comes to the spiritual aspect of our existence.

Such things ought not to be the exception within the house of God!

The power of the Holy Spirit, the gifts of the Holy Spirit, the leading and guidance of God, all these things ought to be a given for believers, for fellowships, for congregations, and for all who name the name of Christ.

If the biggest trick the devil ever pulled was to convince the world he didn't exist, the second biggest trick he ever pulled was to convince the church that it is powerless, and absent of authority.

We have adopted and embraced this victim mentality, wherein "the devil made me do it" becomes our go to motto, and rather than stand and do all to stand, we accept defeat as a given, and as something we are meant to experience as sons and daughters of God.

It is a lie! We are not meant to suffer defeat at the hands of the enemy. We are not meant to be vanquished by the darkness. We are meant to overcome evil, we are meant to overcome the darkness, we are meant to fight against principalities and powers and the rulers of the darkness of this age.

The sad reality is that it's far easier to just sit there, beaten and bruised, telling ourselves there was nothing we could have done, there were no measures we could have taken, and there was no defense we could have mounted, then to actually stand and fight and bleed and thoroughly exhaust oneself.

It is far easier to play the victim, or to blame someone else, than it is to make sure you are ready for battle, that your sword is sharp, and your armor is oiled, that you know what you are doing, and that you stand on the firm ground of knowing who stands with you and fights on your side.

Will God be there if you stand your ground? Most assuredly! That is the comfort and the hope. That is the strength we have in Him: the knowledge that God will be with us, fighting alongside us, and if God is with us, we will surely prevail, we will surely have victory, we will surely overcome any hardship, trial, temptation, or attack.

The question we must ask ourselves, is do we trust God enough to do our part and stand our ground? Do we trust God enough to walk out on the battlefield and make our stand against the enemy?

Certain things are left to us. Certain things are expected of us. God will not do for you or me what we can do for ourselves, and when we are given a command in God's Word, it is wise and prudent that we follow said command to the letter.

> Ephesians 6:10-12, "Finally, my brethren, be strong in the Lord and in the power of His might. Put on the whole armor of God, that you may be able to stand against the wiles of the devil."

Before we can speak on the articles included in our armor, before we can begin to itemize our weapons and our gear, the Bible gives us two clear and undeniable commands.

First, we are told to be strong. Second, we are told to put on the whole armor. If we fail in either of these two prerequisites, knowing what our armor consists of is utterly pointless.

Everything has become a soundbite in this hyperactive generation. We want to jump to the good part. We want to jump to the action. We don't want backstory, we don't want scene setting, just get us to the battle already!

The problem with that kind of thinking is that what you do before the battle, the time you put in preparing for it will likely determine whether you walk off the battlefield on your own two feet, or are carried off.

Some things you just can't hurry. Some things need to be done in the order they were prescribed, otherwise they become pointless exercises in futility.

When we are commanded to be strong we are not commanded to be strong in and of ourselves. We are commanded to be strong in the Lord and in the power of His might. It is His strength flowing through us, the power of His might enveloping us that gives us the necessary wherewithal to stand against the wiles of the devil.

It is not our own strength. It is never in our own strength. Our strength is frail, our skill is lacking, and our prowess in battle leaves much to be desired when we attempt to do battle in our authority rather than God's.

Our second imperative is that we put on the *whole* armor of God. Partial armor just won't cut it. You can't pick and choose what you will put on, and what you will leave behind. Every article in your armor serves a specific purpose and is indispensable.

Most of our armor is meant for defense, while only one of the components is used mainly for attack or offense. While you can show up on the battlefield with half of your armor missing, you will not be long for the battle. Once more I must stress that these actions are imperative, they are not elective. You cannot opt out of putting on your armor. You cannot opt out of being strong in the Lord. The only way is to become a washout, someone who couldn't cut it.

Another aspect of this passage that merits observation is that Paul calls it God's armor. **"Put on the whole armor of God."** What this means is that you can't make your own helmet, you can't make up your own shield, you can't play the amateur metalsmith and forge your own sword. You are assigned and given your armor by God.

We are not some ad hoc militia going to war in homemade leather jerkins with pitchforks and axes as weapons. We are the army of God. There is a dress code. There is a code of conduct. Perhaps more Christians today should start acting like it.

If a soldier shames themselves, it is not just their own person they are shaming. They are also shaming their fellow soldiers and brothers in arms, their commanding officers, and even their general.

We cannot take lightly the armor of God, or being conscripted into the army of God. We bear certain responsibilities. We have certain duties. There are expectations that every soldier must live up to.

Since we are on the topic – albeit tangentially – you can't break bread with the enemy and still call yourself a soldier of God, either. If you are quicker to defend sin and perversion than you are to defend the Word of God, then you are a Christian in name only, and there is no light in you.

We are sanctified, set apart, transformed from the inside out and the outside in, chiseled and molded in the image of God. We are set apart for His purpose and not our own.

Your armor is provided to you. It is God's armor. Your duty is to put it on, and keep it clean, well oiled, and practice until God's armor becomes like a second skin, immediately noticing when something is missing, or when something is not as well maintained as it ought to be.

If your sword needs sharpening, sharpen it. If your shield needs shining, shine it. If your breastplate needs oiling because it's starting to get stiff, then oil it. You are a soldier in God's army. You have duties to perform, and no one will do it for you just because you don't feel like it.

Be a complete Christian. Be a true soldier of the cross. Prepare now for a long, protracted, grueling and exhaustive battle that is sure to come, because the devil won't give up without a fight.

If we begin every day with being strong in the Lord and putting on our armor, we will be able to stand, we will be able to fight, and we will be able to overcome the trickeries of the devil.

I'm not saying we won't get bruised, I'm not saying we won't be tired, I'm not saying we won't get cut, or bleed, or sweat, or stumble, but what I am saying is that God will carry us through it all, and we will have the ultimate victory.

The more prepared a soldier, the more equipped a soldier, the more trained a soldier, the less of a chance he has of being wounded in battle.

We begin each day with Jesus on our hearts, with Jesus on our minds, with Jesus encompassing us, and being a present reality with whom we fellowship and commune. This is how we begin every day with being strong in the Lord.

So what are the weapons to which we, as soldiers of Christ have access to? What are the weapons with which we make war against the darkness?

Ephesians 6:12-17, "For we do not wrestle against flesh and blood, but against principalities, against powers, against the rulers of the darkness of this age, against spiritual hosts of wickedness in the heavenly places. Therefore, take up the whole armor of God, that you may be able to withstand in the evil day, and having done all, to stand. Stand therefore, having girded your waist with truth, having put on the breastplate of righteousness, and having shod your feet with the preparation of the gospel of peace; above all, taking the shield of faith with which you will be able to quench all the fiery darts of the wicked one. And take the helmet of salvation, and the sword of the Spirit, which is the word of God."

There you have it. This is the entire inventory, the entire arsenal to which we, as believers have access. Oddly enough there is no Holy Ghost machine gun, there is no denominational bazooka, and there are no heresy-be-gone grenades.

Given man's advances in weaponry over the last few hundred years, one might look upon this list of weapons and deem it ineffectual, inadequate, and demoted. They may look upon this list of weapons and deem them to be no more than a reliquary of the past, something fun to look at but wholly useless in modern warfare.

This might be the case if we were wrestling against flesh and blood, but I assure you we are not. Our battle is against principalities, and powers, and the rulers of the darkness of this age, and there are no more effective weapons against such than truth, righteousness, the gospel of peace, faith, salvation, and the Word of God.

Truth is a weapon against the darkness. Righteousness is a weapon against the darkness. Faith is a weapon against the darkness. They may not be glamorous to some, they may not entertain as others might like them to, but they are effective, and the enemy fears them.

The enemy is not afraid of showmen. The enemy is not afraid of entertainers. The enemy is not afraid of men and women looking to promote their own agenda, or build their own kingdom.

What the enemy fears is a true believer. He is afraid of someone who understands the importance of these simplistic sounding virtues like truth and faith and righteousness and the Word of God.

In his letter to the Ephesians, Paul is honest and forthright. He does not pull any punches, he does not try to sugarcoat anything, and he informs the church at Ephesus that whether they like it or not, they are at war.

This passage in Ephesians 6 is no less than a declaration of war, and to see it any other way would be the very definition of shortsightedness. Paul warns that if we hope to stand, if we hope to fight, if we hope to overcome we need to put on our armor without a moment's worth of hesitation.

The enemy has thrown down the gauntlet; he has made his intentions crystal clear. If you have committed yourself to truth, if you have committed yourself to light, if you have committed yourself to Christ, you are the devil's sworn enemy and he will seek to destroy you.

Knowing this, would it not be both prudent and wise to do our utmost insofar as preparing for the eventual conflict? Would it not be prudent and wise to believe the Word of God and put on the whole armor that we may be able to withstand the evil day?

There is a lot to unpack in this passage, so we will take it step by step. Even though this chapter is about the weapons at our disposal it is never a bad idea to likewise know why weapons are necessary in the first place, and what it is we are expected to use said weapons against.

The first truth we must acknowledge, and one that many in today's slothful Christianity refuse to address, is that we cannot be inactive. We wrestle! Though it may not be against flesh and blood, we nevertheless wrestle against principalities and powers.

The notion that our existence here on earth is all lollipops and cotton candy after we receive Jesus is lunacy of the highest order.

It is after we receive Jesus that the battle begins, and the more we grow in Him the battle intensifies. Mature Christians are a threat to the devil. A Christian who understands the importance of putting on their armor and keeping it on, a believer who has learned how to use their weapons aggressively and offensively, these are the things that gives Satan nightmares.

Because the Word also identifies who our enemy is, we ought never to be ignorant of who we are doing battle against. It is not a secret, it is not a mystery, it's not as though we're looking around every shrub and tree trying to figure out who we're supposed to be fighting.

Paul identifies no less than four agents of darkness against which we wrestle; four nefarious tips of the same spear which the enemy uses with great skill against the children of God.

1. Principalities

2. Powers

3. Rulers of the darkness of this age

4. Spiritual hosts of wickedness in the heavenly place

These are our enemies. These are our adversaries. These are the four things against which we wrestle, and knowing this, Paul encourages us to take up the whole armor of God that we might withstand in the evil day.

It's not the church down the street, it's not other ministries, it's not other preachers, and it's not other Christians. They are not the enemy but the devil sure does love it when we butt heads, when we stab each other in the back, and when we besmirch one another's reputation.

As long as the devil can keep us distracted as to whom the real enemy is he can gain ground, sneak in unnoticed, and wreak havoc among the children of God. He is a master at throwing out red herrings, and watching the children of God scuttle about distracted, and unaware of his ultimate plan.

Just as a refresher, the devil's ultimate plan is your absolute destruction both spiritual and physical. He doesn't want an alliance, he doesn't want to be your friend, and he doesn't make deals.

By now, I'm sure you've heard the fable of the scorpion and the turtle who are trying to cross a river. In case you haven't, the crux of it is that a scorpion, being a very poor swimmer, asked a turtle to carry him on his back across a river.

After a long drawn out protest pointing out that the scorpion would surely sting it the turtle finally relented and agreed to give the scorpion a ride on its back. The scorpion was convincing and his argument was sound. It insisted it would not sting the turtle due to the undeniable fact that both would sink to the bottom and drown if it did.

Halfway across the river the scorpion stings the turtle, and before going down to the depths the turtle weakly asks, "Why did you sting me? Now both of us will die."

"Because it is my nature", answered the scorpion.

In this story you will always be the turtle, and the devil will always be the scorpion. No matter how logical and reasonable his argument for not harming you might be, no matter how enticing his proposition to make an alliance and learn to get along and coexist, because it is his nature, the devil will strike the mortal blow eventually.

We must adopt the mentality that we either come home "with" our shields or "on" them. This is a battle to the death! It is a battle for eternity, and no one who calls Christ Lord will be able to avoid this battle.

Because you know you have a mortal enemy, because you know his intent, because you will eventually have to stand against him, because it is a certainty that you will see the evil day, put on your armor so you may stand.

What's more, we are taking the fight to the enemy. This is his territory, this is his turf, and he has snares and pits laid about everywhere. We proceed with caution, following our orders to the letter, because only in complete obedience will we be assured of God's protection.

This is the message Paul is attempting to relay, and it is by no means a lighthearted message. He is not insinuating that there is nothing you need do. He is not insinuating that you will not have to exert yourself. He is encouraging one and all to prepare and be ready for the battle is coming their way.

Have you done all to stand? This is the question that often gives me reason for pause, the question that often stirs much contemplation in me.

Have I done all that is within my power to do to stand? Have I prepared sufficiently? Am I sufficiently prayed up? Is all of my armor on? Do I know how to use my weapons?

Some things are incumbent upon us as individuals to do, and putting on our armor is one of those things. Paul does not assert that God will put our armor on for us, he instructs us to put our armor on for ourselves.

By what Paul writes to the church in Ephesus, there are certain things every believer ought to have, and no believer could do without. They are the components that make up the armor of God, the selfsame armor necessary for us in order to make war against the darkness.

1. The band of truth

2. The breastplate of righteousness

3. The shoes of the preparation of the gospel of peace

4. The shield of faith

5. The helmet of salvation

6. The sword of the Spirit

Before we get into the individual articles that make up the whole armor of God there one glaring observation I would be remiss in not making, and that is: of the six Paul lists, five are articles of defense, and only one is a weapon of offense or attack.

All but the sword of the Spirit are meant to protect you, to keep you, to defend you against the enemy, and this fact should not go unnoticed. The primary purpose of the armor of God is your protection. The primary purpose of the armor of God is to keep you from getting wounded or killed on the battlefield.

A faithful soldier will take inventory of their equipment periodically, and make sure that everything they need in the event of battle is ready to be used at a moment's notice.

A faithful soldier knows exactly where his breastplate, helmet, shield, sword, belt and shoes are, for he is never far from them.

Paul takes what was commonly a Roman soldier's battle armor, and spiritualizes it, giving each item a specific spiritual designation. What I've always found interesting and worthy of contemplation was why he chose to couple the virtues with the items the way he did. Why is it not the shield of truth, or the breastplate of salvation? Why those specific designations, to those specific articles?

Some of the designations are easier to associate than others. The helmet of salvation seems readily obvious, since the helmet sits on the head of the soldier, but other designations require contemplation and prayerfulness in order to understand the full magnitude of what Paul is attempting to relay.

1. The Band of Truth

Let's begin with what it means to have our waist girded with truth. Historically speaking, the girding of one's loins was meant to keep someone from stumbling, or being caught off balance by having his tunic grabbed and pulled.

During the time of Paul's writing to the Ephesians, the primary garment was a tunic. It was nothing fancy, just a square piece of cloth with holes cut out for the head and the arms. The one drawback of the tunic was that it was loose, it flowed, and if your waist was not girded, in the eventuality of hand to hand combat, you would be at a disadvantage.

Your opponent could either grab at your loose tunic and pull you off balance, or there was the risk that one might trip over their tunic as they raced into the heat of battle. As such, when battle was about to commence, the soldiers would tuck their tunics in to a thick leather belt, thereby girding their loins.

By studying the ancient armor of Paul's day, the selfsame armor he saw in his mind's eye as he penned these words, one sees that the belt also held the breastplate in place. For those soldiers who were in possession of breastplates, the belt would keep the breastplate tight around the soldier, and prevent it from banging against his chest when in battle.

Spiritually speaking, when your waist is girded with truth you will not stumble. Truth protects you from tripping on the lie, because when you know the truth, the truth has set you free and you have become inoculated against deception.

When we are girded with truth we are above reproach. Truth keeps our integrity intact, and there is not a whiff of hypocrisy in our conduct if we are ever careful to keep ourselves bound by it.

It all begins with truth. The first and most vital part of a Christian's armor is truth. If truth is absent your armor is compromised from the get go. The band or belt of truth serves more than one purpose, and is necessary for more than just keeping one's garments girded. It is also that upon which your sheath and subsequently your sword hangs on.

There are three primary dangers to not having one's waist girded with the belt of truth:

1. Your robe or tunic will trip you up.

2. Your breastplate is not secure.

3. Your sword will drop to the ground.

In order to stand on the day of battle we must not only know the truth but we must also live by the truth.

Without truth being an active, consistent, daily component of our lives, we will not survive the battle, no matter how well prepared we might believe ourselves to be.

Only by possessing truth, and having our waist girded with the belt of truth will the rest of our armor stay on. Without truth, we will get tripped up by the devil's lies, because his lies are well crafted, continuous, and multi-pronged.

The devil knows how to craft a lie. He is the father of lies, and he's been at it for a very long time.

The only way to combat the lie, the only proven means by which we can counteract deception is to possess truth.

Putting on the belt of truth is putting on the truth of the Bible. It is knowing the Word of God. It is this truth, this absolute truth of God's word that keeps the rest of our armor on. Without it, we're just a bunch of discombobulated individuals who make it up as they go along, and fight the battles they choose to fight rather than the battles they are commanded to fight.

2. The Breastplate of Righteousness

The second item in your arsenal is the breastplate of righteousness. Historical context tells us that Roman soldiers wore breastplates on their chest and torso protecting vital organs. Usually made of metal, because they only protected the vitals these breastplates were not cumbersome like a suit of armor would be, and so the soldier could keep his breastplate on for longer than those who would otherwise falter due to weariness.

Historically speaking, many a man perished marching toward a given battle because they gave in to exhaustion due to the heaviness of their suit of armor. Breastplates are not so. The compromise of the breastplate is that you might suffer some cuts or wounds on your extremities, but what it surrenders in protection it more than makes up for in sustainability and ease of movement.

If putting on the belt of truth is *knowing* the Word of God, then putting on the breastplate of righteousness is living the Word of God. Being in possession of the breastplate of righteousness and actually putting it on is the difference between being a Pharisee or a Disciple.

There are many a soul wandering about today who know the Word of God well enough, they possess the head knowledge when it comes to what the Bible says, but they never practically apply it. They never live the knowledge they've amassed. To them it is merely theoretical.

Breastplates are useful for defense. Even when the enemy's slings and arrows get past the shield of faith, they are stopped by the breastplate of righteousness. Righteousness is a protective barrier, and when one is walking in righteousness, every attack of the enemy is readily repelled by the breastplate of righteousness.

Another aspect of the breastplate we must take into account is that it not only protects against frontal assaults it also protects your back from the attacks of traitors and betrayers of the faith.

Having been in ministry for over thirty years I can say with honesty and deep sadness that you will likely suffer as many attacks from individuals you supposed were brothers, as you will from the enemy himself.

Righteousness protects your back as well as your front, it protects you from attacks without the household of faith as well as attacks from within the household of faith.

It is when we deviate from righteousness – when we allow compromise and duplicity to worm its way into our hearts – that cracks and chinks begin to show up in our breastplate, and eventually one of the enemy's attacks will make contact, and penetrate beyond the breastplate.

To put it bluntly, absent righteousness your vital organs are exposed, and what would have otherwise bounced off your breastplate will likely kill you without it.

Righteousness is a barrier against attack, and it is the atmosphere in which we are most pleasing in the sight of God. Righteousness is such an important component of the believer's life that if we seek it and the kingdom of God first, then everything else will work itself out.

As with every other aspect of our spiritual walk, righteousness is not a one-time get-it-done-and-never-think-about-it-again sort of endeavor. Righteousness and the pursuit thereof are constant, ongoing, perpetual aspects of our Christian life, and when we stop living righteousness, when we stop pursuing righteousness, our breastplate begins to lose its protective consistency.

It's not just any old breastplate that we must put on; it is the breastplate of righteousness. When there is specificity in the Word, it is there for a reason. When the Bible drills down on a topic and identifies it beyond generality it is wise and prudent not to gloss over it, but acknowledge its existence and importance rather than brushing it off as semantic.

I realize full well righteousness has fallen out of favor with the church. We would rather speak of self-empowerment and positivity than righteousness because righteousness requires action, and oftentimes righteousness requires that we sacrifice the flesh.

Attaining righteousness and living out one's righteousness on a daily basis is far more difficult than looking in a mirror and repeating the same tired and worn out phrase day in and day out that is meant to do nothing more than appease the flesh or give one a temporary respite from their drudgery.

We put on the breastplate of righteousness by putting it on. There are no shortcuts, no hacks, no special prayers we can pray to make it appear on our bodies. In order to attain it we must practice righteousness, and in order to maintain it righteousness must become part of who we are, not something that we practice on occasion.

3. The Shoes of the Preparation of Peace

Today we call them shoes, back then they called them sandals. Although at first glance the need for footwear might seem redundant since every adult or able bodied individual wears shoes. When we begin to research what it was that Paul meant by putting on the shoes of the preparation of peace, we realize that not all footwear was created equal, even back during Roman times.

There was a marked difference between the sandals of the average citizen, and the sandals of a soldier. Although by all appearances they seemed the same, the soldier's sandals had an added component that oftentimes made all the difference in battle.

A Roman soldier's sandals were fitted with spikes on the bottom of the soles, so that if need be, the soldier could dig in, find purchase, and not give up ground to the enemy.

This one small addition to the soldier's sandals allowed a solider to do what Paul encourages us all to do no less than four times within the span of verses: stand firm!

There is nobility in standing your ground, of not retreating, of not giving up, of not surrendering. Knowing that our enemy takes no prisoners, knowing that the devil gives no quarter, we have no choice but to fight to the end wherever the battle might happen to take place.

We do not choose the terrain of the battle. This is an uncomfortable truth for many a believer, but it is truth nevertheless. We do not choose the time and place when the enemy will engage us, we do not choose the time and place when we will have to make a stand and defend the truth, but by having our feet shod with the preparation of the gospel of peace, we will be able to stand regardless of the terrain.

When a soldier is well equipped, when a soldier possesses all the components that make up his armor, many worries, fears, and concerns are instantly eliminated and the solider can focus on the battle, on defending himself, and beating back the enemy.

Whether you are fighting on dewy grass or uneven terrain, whether the earth beneath your feet is soft or hard becomes irrelevant, because the sandals will give you purchase, they will ground you and give you foundation.

Many believers today cannot find purchase, they are not surefooted, and they oftentimes stumble because their feet are not shod with the preparation of the gospel of peace.

Standing and having done all to stand is required of every soldier of Jesus. We cannot blame God for our defeats, we cannot blame God for our failures, we cannot blame God for losing a battle if we have not firstly done what we were commanded to do, and prepared to the best of our ability for the inevitability of war.

It's not God's fault that I am slothful; it's not God's fault that I am easily distracted; it's not God's fault that I chose to pursue other things during the time I was given than to prepare for battle.

The Word of God is very clear: do this and you will not stumble. Do this and you will not fall. Do this and you will not falter. Do this and you will be victorious over the enemy. Put on the whole armor of God. Do this and you will be more than a conqueror.

Men's lack of proficiency with the spiritual weapons they've been allotted cannot be blamed on God, nor can their lack of preparedness.

Yes, it would be a far easier thing if we can blame others for our shortcomings, it would be a far easier thing if we could blame others for our ill preparedness, but some responsibility for why the household of faith suffers so much defeat must fall squarely on the shoulders of the household of faith.

We cannot dismiss and discount the specific instructions that are guaranteed to bring about victory, go about fighting the fight the way we think it ought to be fought, and blame our General when we are felled by the enemy.

In order to have our feet shod with the preparation of the gospel of peace, we must first identify what the gospel of peace is.

We know by way of study that *gospel* means good news.

Now that we've identified what the gospel means, we drill down a bit further to discover what the *good news* is.

Contrary to the belief of some, the good news is not that God wants to make you rich, or give you a plane, or straighten your teeth, or clear your acne. The good news is that while God is holy and we were lost, He loved us so completely, He loved us with such passion, that He sent His only begotten Son to die on a cross that we might be reconciled unto Him.

Now that we understand the full meaning of the word gospel, we can also understand why Paul calls it the gospel of peace. It is called the gospel of peace because God made peace with us through the death of His Son Jesus on the cross. No other sacrifice would do and God knew this.

Just as the sandals helped keep soldiers on their feet in battle, being prepared to share the Gospel, or as Paul puts it 'having your feet shod with the preparation of the gospel of peace', will help you stay on your feet as a Christian.

It is difficult, if not outright impossible, to share with others what you don't full grasp or understand yourself. I do not know all the ins and outs of thermal dynamics, and so I would never endeavor to explain it to someone else. I know it has to do with the science of heat and temperature and their relation to energy, but that's broad stroking something that is infinitely more complicated.

As saved and sanctified believers, as soldiers in the army of God, we must be ever ready to define, explain, and expound upon the gospel of peace, what it means, what it has done in our lives, and what it can do in the lives of those who would listen.

When your feet are shod you have the assurance that you will not slip, and that your feet will not fly out from under you. You have purchase. You are grounded, and you know where you stand.

When we apply this spiritually, we must be ever ready to explain salvation and defend the gospel, and do it in such a way wherein the enemy can't trip us up.

As a child of God you are a walking, talking, breathing, living recruitment billboard. Men ought to be able to look at you and see something markedly different, and when they inquire of you, you must be able to present the message of the gospel with passion and conviction.

4. The Shield of Faith

The shield of faith is where historical context becomes intriguing, interesting, and eye opening. When Paul speaks of a shield, it's not just any shield, but the Roman shield, which was also known as "the door" due to its massive size.

Any student of history will tell you that each empire, each civilization, each conquering army had their own specific type of shields. For the Huns, who did most of their fighting on horseback, the shields had to be small and compact so as to not burden the horse with more weight than necessary. For the Scots and the English, their shields had to be large and heavy due to the swords they fought with, namely the broadsword.

Because the Roman army was comprised largely of foot soldiers and their greatest asset was discipline and not breaking rank when confronted with the enemy, their shields were very large – almost as tall as a man – and oftentimes it was planted before the soldier and fixed into the earth. Essentially if you had a handful of these shields planted into the earth before you, you had created a wall, a barrier, something that was very difficult to penetrate.

Faith is your wall. Faith is your first line of defense against the enemy, and this is why Paul calls it the shield of faith. If your faith is as it ought to be, if you possess the shield of faith, then a disproportionately large percentage of the time, your shield is as far as the enemy is going to get.

The shield is meant to quench the fiery darts of the enemy, and though in the age of lasers, rockets, and machine guns, fiery darts might not seem like such an imposing threat, they were the most advanced and dangerous weapon of Paul's day.

The reasons fiery darts – or arrows if you search out the Greek translation – were so dangerous is threefold.

1. Fiery darts are difficult to see coming.

2. Fiery darts are fast moving.

3. Fiery darts explode on impact.

Yes, even in Paul's day they had invented arrows that had a lit tip, and they would explode on impact causing far more damage than an average arrow would.

When you think about it, these fiery darts of which Paul speaks describe the enemy's attacks very, very well. The enemy is an experienced enough adversary that he does not telegraph his movements. You don't see him coming from a mile away, but you notice him when he is staring you in the eye, having already begun his attack against you. Hence the importance of always keeping one one's armor, and keeping up one's shield.

Due to the size of the shield, due to the amazing resilience and power of faith, you don't have to see every fiery arrow coming your way, you just hear it thump against your shield and know that once more your faith has protected you.

It's only when your shield is down and you are peppered with a dozen fiery arrows in a breath's time that you realize just how much the shield of faith protected you from, and just how necessary it is for the believer on a daily basis.

Yes, sometimes the shield of faith gets heavy, yes sometimes the shield of faith may seem cumbersome, but all we need keep at the forefront of our minds to nevermore murmur about having to carry it consistently. How often and in how many circumstances has it saved our life!

We also know by their very nature that fiery arrows are fast moving. The enemy notches an arrow, draws back his bow, aims, and lets fly. Things happen in slow motion only in the movies. In real life, in the heat of battle, the speed and fierceness of the enemy's attacks are oftentimes shocking even for veteran warriors and experienced soldiers.

When an adversary's attack is nothing more than a blur in your peripheral vision, that is when you must trust your armor, your weapons, and your training. Defensive action becomes instinctive, as does mounting a counteroffensive. One does not have time to sit and plan on the battlefield, one does not have time to second guess or reevaluate, the only thing that can be done on the battle field is to either act or react, and do your utmost to survive.

Even when soldiers were aware of the first two dangers of the attacks of the enemy some suffered severe wounds due to their ignorance of the third. Fiery arrows explode on impact. Every attack the enemy mounts against you is intended to make a mess. The enemy does not care about collateral damage, the enemy doesn't care about casualties, and the enemy does not care whether or not you get maimed, permanently scarred, or die outright.

The enemy's single purpose is to incapacitate you, to make you irrelevant as far as the battle is concerned, and if he can cause others to be wounded due to your incapacitation, all the better. This is largely the reason the enemy goes after leaders, preachers, pastors, and evangelists more than the average foot soldier, because he knows that if he can fell one of these, then the collateral damage will extend beyond that one individual.

When a big name falls, when a big name is felled, the ripple effect is evident throughout Christendom. Tragically there are even other believers whose faith is shaken if not altogether shattered by the fall of someone they deemed spiritually superior to themselves. We have witnessed this time and again, and it never gets easier to stomach.

So what are these fiery darts, exactly? We speak of them in general terms well enough, but what are the fiery darts the enemy employs against the children of God?

Unfortunately, the list is long but I will list a handful just so we can better understand how ruthless and underhanded the enemy is.

1. Pride

2. Fear

3. Temptation

4. Greed

5. Lust

6. Doubt

7. Duplicity

As I said, the list is long, and each individual is more susceptible to one arrow than to others, and as the enemy is a brilliant tactician he knows your weakness, he knows where you are vulnerable, and that is where He will attack.

He will not attack with greed someone whose weakness is lust, nor will he attack someone whose weakness is pride with fear. The reason the enemy's attacks are so dangerous for believers is because he knows what weapons to employ to best hurt you as an individual. This is likewise the reason the shield of faith must always be before you, as Paul says *"above all"* so that it protects you continually.

The shield of faith stops the fiery darts of the enemy before they can do any damage to your person. It is so complete, so imposing, so protective, that the only way to get spiritually wounded is by dropping our shield.

When we drop our shield, the arrows drop us. This simple truth ought to be sobering enough to keep us ever vigilant and on guard.

Seeing as the shield is such an important part of the Christian's armor, and that keeping one's shield up is of paramount importance the question remains: how do we keep our shield up?

How can a believer live in an atmosphere of faith – essentially living by faith – so that his shield is never down, so that he is never without the protection of the shield of faith?

The simple answer is by believing what God says above what anyone else says, and living out that belief in a practical manner, consistently. One does not live by faith by having one experience with God, one does not live by faith by raising a hand at a crusade, nor does one live by faith by attending a church service every other week. One lives by faith by establishing a relationship with God, obeying God, serving God, and submitting to the authority of God in all things.

Amazing things happen in our lives when we begin to trust God implicitly. We trust God, therefore we do not fear man. We trust God, therefore we do not fear the devil. We trust God, therefore we do not fear our own shortcomings or inclinations. We trust God, therefore we have nothing to fear.

Your shield is up as long as your faith remains tethered in Christ, as long as you remain in a state of obedience and trust, knowing that He will never forsake you, leave you, or lead you astray.

Faith in God is your shield, and it is the God in whom you have placed your faith that ultimately protects you.

Proverbs 30:5, "Every word of God is pure; He is a shield to those who put their trust in Him."

5. The Helmet of Salvation

As far as historical context is concerned, the Roman helmets in Paul's time were made of either bronze or iron, and they protected the neck, the head, and much of the soldier's face.

The helmet is designed to protect the one vital organ that the breastplate does not, and is indispensable in battle. Since a helmet is easy to put on most soldiers only wore them when battle was imminent, or when they found themselves in formation in anticipation of battle. Most Roman helmets had a metal ring at the very top so it could be hung by a hook on the soldier's armor. In this fashion, although one didn't have to wear the helmet continuously, they always knew where it was, and that it was within easy reach.

There are a handful of spiritual components we need to discuss regarding the helmet of salvation so as not to create confusion, or absence of clarity.

The first and most important thing regarding the helmet of salvation is that you do not become saved because you put on the helmet of salvation. You have the helmet of salvation because you are saved.

No man can barter, buy, or steal the helmet of salvation from another and claim it as their own. It belongs to God, and He distributes it to those who are saved as part of their armor and readiness for battle.

> Isaiah 59:17, "For He put on righteousness as a breastplate, and a helmet of salvation on His head; He put on the garments of vengeance for clothing, and was clad with zeal as a cloak."

Just as there are consequences for misplacing, misappropriating, or misusing one's assigned weapons and uniform in any branch of the armed services, there are consequences in the spiritual as well.

In today's church we are repeatedly told that there is neither a code of conduct among the soldiers of God, nor is there any implied responsibility on the part of the believer to make certain that once they've been assigned the armor of God they maintain it in the same condition and resplendence it was received.

We are continually bombarded with teaching and doctrine insisting that slothfulness, duplicity, compromise, indecision, and absence of sanctification have now become the norm and as such God can have no realistic expectation of our living up to the standard He established in His Word.

Believers, especially newborn babes who have not as yet seen the first sign of battle, are made to feel at ease when they treat the armor of God haphazardly, or dismiss it altogether because it is constricting, uncomfortable, or too much to worry about.

"You forgot your sword and your shield? Well, that's okay, you can throw rocks at the devil or kick dirt in his eye."

THE BATTLE-READY BELIEVER

Showing up ill prepared on the battlefield is the quickest way to ensure one's demise. It is because we underestimate the fierceness and intent of our enemy that we can be so flippant about our armor. It is because we underestimate the abilities of our enemy that we can be so disinterested when it comes to learning how to do spiritual warfare, and stand against the darkness.

Some men are only brave when others bleed in their stead, but as a child of God you do not have that luxury!

You cannot send someone to do battle on your behalf; you cannot conscript nor can you hire someone to stand against the enemy and confront him. You have to stand. You have to fight. You have to do battle because salvation is an individual experience, not a collective enterprise.

Men love to be coddled not realizing it is impeding their growth and their maturity. Men love to be coddled not realizing that the absence of correction, the absence of structure, and the absence of discipline is detrimental to their spiritual wellbeing.

The helmet of salvation protects your mind against doubt. Whenever the enemy comes in like a flood attempting to catch you off balance or sow doubt into your mind, the helmet rebuffs his attempts and keeps you on the solid foundation of the Gospel.

In the real world there is an undeniable correlation between individuals who take too many lumps to the head and brain damage. We have seen it in boxers, in football players, and pretty much any other sport or enterprise wherein the head takes a lot of punishment.

There is also a correlation in the spiritual, wherein individuals who have taken one too many blows to the head without the protection of the helmet of salvation begin to believe things that have no scriptural basis or foundation.

6. The Sword of the Spirit

We have arrived at the one component of the Christian's armor that is primarily a weapon of offense rather than something used for defense or protection. While the other five components of the armor are primarily for defensive purposes, the sword of the spirit is the one component with which we attack the enemy, and with which we take the fight to devil.

For anyone who is a history buff – even an amateur history buff like myself – it would be tantamount to heresy not to delve into the historical context of the sword, which Paul likely used as the prototype when referring to the sword of the Spirit.

By no means am I a swordsmith, but as a boy growing up swords intrigued me. From the saber, to the broadsword, to the foils and rapiers, to the longswords, to the scimitars, and the subcategories that make up the world of swords, one realizes that each culture had its own version of the sword, a version that was very geographically specific.

While the Asian populace preferred the lighter swords, the katana and the tan-to being most popular and widely known, the Nordic tribes preferred the longer, heavier broadswords or long swords.

What the Roman army used during the days of Paul was a sword known as the gladius, or the short sword. The Roman short sword was brutal and efficient. It was double edged, made of iron, and had a pommel at the end for better grip as well as for hitting one's enemy on the backswing. It was far shorter than the barbarian swords of the time, no more than two feet in length, but pound for pound the gladius was a brutal weapon.

The gladius was the standard issue infantry weapon for the Roman infantryman and is believed to have been adopted by the Romans from Spanish mercenaries during the first Punic war. The gladius was so successful, and the soldiers who grew proficient in its use so lethal, that it saw service in the Roman armies for some 250 years. There is a reason the gladius is called the sword that conquered the world and it's not because it was a fashion statement or something to be kept unused and gathering dust.

Having seen firsthand how complete a weapon this double edged sword was, when Paul writes about the sword of the Spirit it is within the historical context of the gladius. This was not a fencing foil he was referencing; it was an imposing, capable weapon.

The soldiers of the time were most often taught and trained to thrust or stab rather than cut or slash. There is a far better chance of striking a killing blow when you stab or thrust than when you cut or slash, and in battle, when everything is on the line, your mission is not to give your enemy a paper cut, it is to kill the enemy before he has a chance of killing you.

If your enemy desires to kill you and all you desire in return is to hurt his feelings, he will vanquish you because your response to his actions are neither measured nor equal. Every time we approach battle it must be with an *all or nothing* mindset. Anything less gives us an excuse to not do all to stand, and to not do all the exert ourselves to the uttermost in the fight.

These are not war games; this is war. This is not a reenactment of some battle or some skirmish; it's the real thing.

There are a handful of instances wherein great military minds, generals of renown, ordered their ships burned upon landing so that in the mind of his men there would be no possibility of retreat. From William of Normandy, to Emperor Julian, to Cortez, these men eliminated every option save two: victory or death.

When we bring this into the spiritual sphere it simply means not to take it easy on the devil because he will never take it easy on you. Don't pull your punches. Don't pull your blows. Aim to destroy the enemy every time you stand on the battlefield. Having this thought at the forefront of our minds every time we exercise, our proficiencies will go a long way toward our fighting in this manner during actual battle.

So what is the sword of the Spirit? When we answer this question, we know what it is we are supposed to take up. Paul gives us a strong indication as to what the Sword of the Spirit is. In fact, he comes right out and tells us that the sword of the Spirit is the Word of God.

Even with such a straightforward definition of what the sword of the Spirit is, there are many misconceptions within the church today, and many interpretations that stretch beyond the Word of God.

Contrary to the belief of some, the sword of the Spirit is neither the Spirit of God, nor is it your physical Bible. Although the latter could be deduced from Paul's definition, the former just has no Biblical anchor. As I said, although the sword of the Spirit is the Word of God, it is not your physical Bible.

In order to understand what the sword of the Spirit is, we must get a bit scholarly and define and dissect the meaning of two Greek words, and the difference between them.

The two words we must define if we are to understand what the sword of the Spirit is, are Logos, and Rhema. Since this is not a scholarly tome on the original Greek writings of Scripture, or a hermeneutics course on the differentiation and deviation of nuanced interpretations, I will endeavor to keep it as simple as possible.

Logos refers to the entire written Word of God, from cover to cover, complete, intact and unabridged.

Rhema refers to individual verses, scripture passages, sometimes whole chapters within the Bible, but not the complete, intact, and unabridged Word of God.

In the original Greek, when Paul tells us to "take up the sword of the Spirit, which is the word of God", he uses Rhema rather than Logos. As such the passage would read, "take up the sword of the Spirit, which is the **Rhema** of God."

Simply owning a Bible gives you the Sword of the Spirit like putting on a spandex suit give you super powers. It simply doesn't happen, and those who insist upon this are misled, and teaching a faux gospel. It is knowing the Bible that gives you the sword of the Spirit, and once you know it, once it has become alive in your heart, you can actively use your sword to do battle against the darkness.

When we acknowledge the reality that knowing the Word of God bequeaths us the Sword of the Spirit we realize that there are countless swords within the Word of God that we can use against the enemy, and not just one. There are many applications for your word, there are many ways you can use it to strike a blow against the enemy.

We will get into the details of how to successfully use the Sword of the Spirit against the enemy further in this chapter, but first I would be remiss if I did not reemphasize its importance in the life of the believer.

The Sword of the Spirit is the only thing that can destroy the enemy! That statement alone ought to be enough to galvanize us to action, not only to make sure we possess the Sword of the Spirit but also that we know how to wield it properly.

Absent the Sword of the Spirit in our arsenal we are perpetually on the defensive, but because we lack the necessary weapon we never go on the offensive against the enemy. In such a case the best we can hope for is that we do not give up any territory or ground to the adversary, but we can never hope to take ground from him.

At best our battle becomes a stalemate, but because it is likely that the enemy has far more stamina than we do, if we do not possess the Sword of the Spirit, eventually we will tire of deflecting slings and fiery arrows, eventually we will tire of raising our shield, and the enemy will get a blow in that will either incapacitate us or fell us altogether.

Your sword is your lifeline in battle. Lose your sword, and you will likely lose your life. It is that serious. It is that final.

> Isaiah 27:1, "In that day the Lord with His severe sword, great and strong, will punish the Leviathan the fleeing serpent, and He will slay the reptile that is in the seal."

If the Sword of the Spirit which we are given belongs to God, then it is no intellectual leap or stretch of the imagination to say that we possess the selfsame sword, and are able to inflict the selfsame damage to the enemy.

If we have the same sword in our possession as God Himself wields, then why aren't we using it, or if we are using it, why are we not using it to the extent of effectiveness the Bible clearly tells us it possesses?

As previously stated there are countless ways to use your sword both as a weapon of attack against the enemy as well as a weapon of defense against the enemy's attacks.

What follows is just a handful of examples, and by no means all the ways we can use the Sword of the Spirit.

Using your sword to attack the enemy:

1. Rebuke the devil and he will flee.

2. Cast evil spirits out of individuals

3. Speak comfort to those in despair.

4. Speak truth to those in deception.

5. Speak strength to those who are weak.

6. Speak boldness to those who are fearful.

7. Speak hope to those who are hurting.

8. Speak Jesus to those who are seeking.

Using your sword to defend against the enemy's attacks:

1. Stand on the promises of God:

   My God is faithful!

   My God shall supply all my needs!

   My God knows my struggle!

   I am not forsaken!

   I am more than a conqueror!

2. Speak the Scriptures when attacked:

When tempted to do evil – **Romans 12:21, "Do not be overcome with evil, but overcome evil with good."**

When feeling overwhelmed – **2 Chronicles 20:15, "Thus says the Lord to you: 'Do not be afraid nor dismayed because of this great multitude, for the battle is not yours, but God's.'"**

When facing the enemy – **Psalm 18:39, "For You have armed me with strength for battle."**

Unless you know the Word of God, you cannot wield it with proficiency. There are no hacks, there are no shortcuts, we must get into the Word every day, and it must be a personal, intimate, consistent practice in our lives if we hope to grow our skill level.

Reading the Bible once and safely tucking it away nevermore to be revisited will not give you the necessary proficiency to defeat the enemy. Knowing a verse or two that appealed to you at any given moment but disregarding entire swaths of scripture, will not give you the necessary proficiency in battle.

A Christian must be disciplined just as a solider must be disciplined and hone his skills every single day in anticipation for battle.

There are five surefire ways to build up our arsenal as well as our proficiency with the Sword of the Spirit.

1. Immersion!

2. Daily Bible reading!

3. Verse memorization!

4. Meditation on Scripture!

5. Application of Scripture in warfare!

If we practice these five things consistently, we will become a devastating weapon against the enemy and his minions. It is men who not only possess but know how to wield the weapons in their arsenal that the enemy fears and knows by name.

One of the first thing they teach you in basic training, once you've enlisted and showed up for boot camp, is to never point the muzzle of your weapon at fellow soldiers, or men assigned to your unit.

Although most young men and women who've been around guns know this to be an overarching truth from early youth, others who have never held a weapon will oftentimes do cringe worthy things like wave a loaded gun around, not caring where the muzzle is pointing.

This selfsame principle applies to the soldiers of God, and the believers who are preparing to do battle against the darkness: Your sword is to be used against your enemy, not against your fellow brothers in arms.

There are likely more casualties within the household of faith due to friendly fire, than there are from direct attacks of the enemy. It is far easier for some to strike out at their fellow brothers, because they are unsuspecting of such attacks and are blindsided, than it is to stand against the enemy, confront him, and make war against him.

The Word of God, your sword, is a two-edged weapon, and as such it is paramount that you know what you are doing when you wield it. Because it is a two-edged blade, you are just as likely to hurt yourself as you are to hurt the enemy if you don't know what you are doing, and are not proficient in wielding it.

There is one other component that Paul mentions in his writings on the armor of God, and though not technically one of the pieces that make up the armor, it is, nevertheless, imperative, and that is prayer.

> *Ephesians 6:18-20, "Praying always with all prayer and supplication in the Spirit, being watchful to this end with all perseverance and supplication for all the saints – and for me, that utterance may be given to me, that I may open my mouth boldly to make known the mystery of the gospel, for which I am an ambassador in chains; that in it I may speak boldly as I ought to speak."*

If the Sword of the Spirit is your lifeline in battle, prayer is your line of communication with your general. In order to receive instruction, in order to receive commands, in order to be sent where your general needs you and do what your general needs you to do, prayer must be constant in your life.

Throughout the Bible we see prayer as being the one unifying attribute of all the great men of God. Even to our modern era, wherein we hear of giants of the faith who were able to do great exploits for the kingdom, the one commonality these men shared was prayer.

Though they might hail from different continents, though they might speak different languages, though they might vary in age, level of intelligence and upbringing, prayer seems to be the recurring theme in the lives of those who stand out within the household of faith, those to whom we look up and respect for their selflessness and tenacity.

If the enemy can sever your line of communication with God, if he can keep you from daily prayer by some form or another, then it's only a matter of time before he can feed you false information, before he can lead you to a place wherein you find yourself alone, removed from your battalion, outnumbered, and easily felled.

Ask any soldier who has seen combat, ask any soldier who has had to depend upon open lines of communication, and they will tell you how indispensable they are.

One of the greatest coups by the allied forces during the second World War came when they were able to break the German cypher known as Enigma, thereby reading their communications and being made aware of subsequent invasions, the positioning of German U-boats, and countless others secrets the Germans thought impregnable because of their device.

As long as your line of communication with God is open, the devil cannot break God's cypher. As long as you prayerfully wait on the Lord for instruction, guidance, leading, and specificity you will be a sure footed soldier, one who does not hesitate, one who does not second guess, and one who does not doubt his position or his mission.

The topic of prayer cannot be contained in a handful of paragraphs, nor can one solitary book do it justice. As such, if you do not know how to pray, if you need help in understanding the importance of prayer, there are countless resources out there wherein you can immerse yourself in the study of prayer and learn all there is to learn about it.

Prayer, fasting, reading the Word, knowing the Word, speaking the Word, all these are the ways by which the warrior trains, and the more one trains consistently and judiciously, the more proficient they become in the use of their arsenal. It is the same with anything in this life. The more time one puts into achieving their desired goal, the closer they come to achieving it. Any learned skill takes time to perfect, and it is in the perfecting that the true mastery of one's skill comes into focus.

Some warriors become so proficient in the use of their weapons that it is tantamount to an art form. Just watching the fluidity of motion, the nimbleness with which they go through their routine, reminds one of an exquisite ballet, something to be respected for the time it took to achieve.

I have one final thought about the armor of God, and that is this: You only take off the armor when the battle is done, and not before. There is no respite for the battle ready believer. The enemy we face will never agree to a ceasefire, and so we will never have a season of rest.

Likewise, there is no leave to be had in the army of God. We don't get to take a few weeks off just to go fishing and decompress. The enemy does not have a code of honor, he has no code of ethics, so if he sees your guard down at any moment in your life, it is then that he will choose to launch his most brutal of attacks.

CHAPTER EIGHT

DO YOU KNOW YOUR GENERAL?

Some time ago I was asked to teach a Sunday morning Bible study in a friend's church. After a time of prayer, I chose to teach on the parable of the ten virgins, five who were wise, and five who were foolish. There were about thirty people in attendance, and as the teaching progressed, I could see I was connecting with most of them.

As I got to the part about the five wise virgins refusing to share their oil with the five foolish virgins, a lady started waving her hand and as I acknowledged her, she stood up and said, "I don't think that was very nice of the five wise virgins. I don't feel that was very loving of them."

I proceeded to explain that all ten virgins had the same amount of time to prepare for the groom's arrival, and if five of them chose not to prepare adequately it was not the responsibility of the others to put themselves in danger just because the foolish virgins had been indifferent and unprepared. I then proceeded to emphasize the importance of personal accountability, and the need for individual preparation and sanctification.

It seemed that my answer was satisfactory, because the lady didn't have any follow up questions, and as I was coming to the end of the lesson, I emphasized the fact that the five virgins who had gone to buy oil from those who sold it, had missed out on the groom's arrival, and as consequence were shut out of the wedding.

The selfsame lady that interrupted earlier started waving her hand again, and after once more acknowledging her, she cleared her throat and said, "in my humble opinion what the groom did wasn't right. They were all virgins after all, and that had to account for something."

I'm usually a nice person. I really am. However, something happened that morning. Maybe it was just too early, or I hadn't had enough coffee, or perhaps I'd heard *'in my humble opinion'* one too many times in regards to the absolute Word of God, but I looked at the lady and said in the most soothing voice I could muster, "when it comes to the Bible madam, your opinion or my opinion, humble or otherwise, is irrelevant."

"Well that's just rude", she muttered and sat back down.

Of the estimated six billion people walking the earth today, everyone has an opinion on something, and most have an opinion on everything. Opinions have been likened to many things, and I'm sure you can think of at least one thing that opinions have been likened to.

I don't mind opinionated people. You can have an opinion about the weather, the color blue, whether it should be mandatory that you eat with chopsticks in a Chinese restaurant, but what we are not allowed an opinion on are the established fundamentals of the Gospel.

What we are not allowed an opinion on was whether God was right about a certain thing, or whether or not we could have done it better ourselves given the chance.

It always amazes me when people inquire what my opinion is regarding something that the Bible is very clear on. How can I have an opinion in opposition to the Word, when I am a follower of the Word?

How can I not call sin, sin, and righteousness, righteousness, if God calls them as such?

We have diluted ourselves into believing that we will somehow change the mind of God simply because we feel, think, or have a different opinion than what the Gospel declares as truth. As such, we have transformed that which is absolute into something relative. We have transformed that which is established and eternal, into something subjective and trivial.

This goes beyond second guessing Scripture – which in itself is horrendous and tragic – to second guessing God, and questioning His commands upon the battlefield.

When we disregard God's commands on the battlefield, we not only endanger ourselves, we endanger those in our battalion, those who are counting on us as we count on them to have their backs. If the household of faith does not learn to fight as a single unit, as one formation with one purpose and one clear directive, I fear the enemy will have an easy time dismantling the church when it comes right down to it.

History is rife with individuals who overestimated their skills, who thought themselves superior soldiers to the point of disregarding the orders of their commanding officers, and though we might like to think such practices are relegated to the past, they have blossomed into an epidemic in our day and age.

Yes, there are men who think they know better than God, or assume that just because they believe a thing, God has to automatically go along with it and condone their behavior, their decision, their thought process, or their endeavor.

This sort of mentality is not exclusive to the pew warmers, but even those in leadership. Men and women who claim to be generals in God's army will second guess God, and the word of

God with horrific regularity, as though there will be no consequence or repercussion to their action.

What's worse is that today's average Christian tends to gravitate toward such individuals, showering them with praise and adulation for their twisting and reinterpreting of God's Word to the point that they make it out to say the complete opposite of what it actually says.

I have often sat in stunned silence as I watched one televangelist after another butcher the Word of God to the point of it being unrecognizable, to the roaring applause of those sitting in the audience, as though what these men had just said were not aberrant, as though it were not falsehood, as though it were not heresy.

Many of us today need to reacquaint ourselves with the words of the Lord Jesus. We must once more allow them to take root in our heart, allowing them to grow and blossom.

> Matthew 24:35, "Heaven and earth will pass away, but My words will by no means pass away."

When it comes to the Word, expressions such as 'I feel, I think, or in my humble opinion' should be stricken from our parlance. It doesn't matter what I think, it doesn't matter how I feel, all that matters is what the Word of God says on any given topic or subject. Either I submit myself to the Word of God, or I am in open rebellion.

The same can be said of those times when God gives a specific instruction, a specific command, but we choose to drag our feet and pull at threads and try to circumvent obedience at any cost. In battle, one cannot do as he pleases. In battle, one cannot make up the rules as they go along, they cannot choose their place, nor can they choose their rank. In battle everyone obeys their commanding officer, their general, they go where they are told, they fight when they are told to fight, and they advance when they are told to advance.

We fight under the banner of truth with God as our general, and though some choose to fall by the wayside or become traitors to the cause, we who remain must be ever vigilant and ready to defend the Gospel.

I will put this as plainly as possible: **You cannot obey the Scriptures without obeying God, and you cannot obey God without obeying the Scriptures!**

If we choose to obey the counsel of God, then we must obey the whole counsel of God, and not cherry pick only the things we like. If we choose to obey the Scriptures, then we must obey the Scriptures in their entirety, including those passages the flesh finds difficult to fall in line with, or those truths which man has rebelled against since the beginning of time.

Truth remains truth regardless of what I believe, regardless of how I feel about it, or that my opinion differs from that of the Word. It is the pinnacle of pride and arrogance to assume that what we think, or how we feel takes preeminence over the written Word of God, or that He will overlook our rebellion and disobedience, simply because we weren't on the same page as Him, and we considered His ways too extreme, and too constrictive.

It simultaneously amazes me and frightens me how readily men can appropriate God's authority, and establish their own righteousness rather than submit to the righteousness of God. We've started throwing around titles like *'casual Christianity'*, as though there were such thing, and wonder why the churches are in such disarray, why we no longer see miracles, why we no longer hear the voice of God clearly, why there is such confusion and why the love of many is growing so cold.

Spiritual weekend warriors are a danger to the Body of Christ, because they know not of discipline, they know not of training, but most of all because they know not of obedience regardless of the command.

It is time to get serious about the Word of God. It is time to open our eyes to the reality of the times we are living in, it is time that we stopped playing church, and it is time to get right with God. My duty before an omnipotent and omniscient God is not to mollycoddle you but to speak the truth of His word to you. My duty before He who knows all is not to water down or dilute the gospel to suit a lazy and indifferent generation, but to present you with the reality of the battle we are embroiled in, and the need to know the voice of your General and obey it without question or hesitation.

You dear friend have a duty of your own: to either receive and accept the word of God, or to reject it. I know I will do my part until I am no longer able, because as Paul once admonished every believer to do, I run my race in such a way that I might obtain the prize. I love you in Jesus; this is why I tell the truth to you. I love you in Jesus; this is why I will stand on the Word of God, and write truth even at the risk of alienating you. Your soul is far too precious to God to play games with.

I pray we do not view the Word through the prism of human sensibilities, or human emotion, but through the prism of God's truth. I pray we do not choose obedience toward our General based on whether or not we would give the same command given similar circumstances, because our ways are not as His ways, and His thoughts are not as our thoughts.

I have no right or authority to question God, first because He is God, and second because I do not see the battlefield as He sees it. His vantage point is very different than my own, and though something might not make sense to me at that particular moment, it will become clear at a later date.

I know the flesh doesn't like to hear it but God sees more than you do, knows more than you do, and can do more than you can. We stand in service to God in a spirit of humility, openness and obedience, not one of contrarianism and confrontation. There are far too many treasonous souls calling themselves believers today, and they are dismantling the household of faith brick by brick.

As I stated, I believe men and women today are appropriating God's authority and establishing their own righteousness rather than submitting to the righteousness of God.

Romans 10:3, "But they being ignorant of God's righteousness, and seeking to establish their own righteousness, have not submitted to the righteousness of God."

Today men and women, who by their own assertion are supposed servants of God, and followers of Christ, are following in the footsteps of those Paul called ignorant of God's righteousness, dismissing and resisting the will of God thereby establishing their own righteousness.

In order to submit to God, we must first mortify pride and humble ourselves, and this is the most difficult aspect of what I like to call the discipline of submission for countless souls.

Blinded by our own sense of self-worth, by our overestimation of our own wisdom, we rebel against He who is the source of wisdom, and as stiff necked and stubborn sons of disobedience we refuse to submit to the authority of God.

"We have found a better way; we have found an easier way; we have found a simpler way;" these are the cries of the rebellious heart, the heart which is unwilling to bend its knee, and yield itself to the will of God.

The Bible tells us that there is only one way, there is only one truth, and there is only one life, and that is Jesus Christ. Men may have found easier ways, men may have found simpler ways, but they are not ways that lead to the kingdom of heaven. They are not ways that lead to the kingdom of God. They are not ways that lead to victory in battle or to the crown of the overcomer that awaits those who endure to the end.

Although the starting point of rebellion differs from one individual to another, some seeking justification for sins, others simply dismissing the commandments of God, others still refusing to believe the fundamentals of scripture, the end result is always the same. Regardless of where disobedience and rebellion begin, the end result is being left to the desires of our wicked hearts, deceived into believing that the god of our making will save us in the day of battle.

> *James 4:7, "Therefore submit to God. Resist the devil and he will flee from you."*

This admonition comes at the end of a lengthy rebuke, one, which if preached in many churches today would be grounds for dismissal of the pastor for having so offended and psychologically damaged his congregation.

Among the choice words used to describe the designated readers of the epistle of James, they are called adulterers and adulteresses, murderers, covetous idolaters, lustful creatures who desire the friendship of the world, knowing full well this will mean enmity with God. James simply holds up the mirror of God's truth, and describes the reflections he sees within what ought to be the congregation of the saints.

The cure for their condition was a combination of two necessary attributes every Christian ought to possess. James admonished all who would heed his warning to repent, and to submit to God.

All the evils that had befallen those to whom he was writing, and unfortunate as it might be we see the selfsame evils alive and well in many churches today, were the root cause of pride and haughtiness. They thought themselves wise in their own understanding, and as such refused to submit to the authority of God. They bypassed obedience on the battlefield and trusted in their own understanding rather than in the wisdom of God.

We cannot hope to be fruitful, we cannot hope to obtain peace, and we cannot hope to live in victory, or have a full Christian life without submitting to God.

The Word is very clear on the topic of yielding ourselves, of submitting ourselves to God, but nothing is more contradictory to human nature than submission. It is only when we submit; when our will and God's will are one, that we obtain those illusive attributes such as peace, joy, and comfort.

Where there is no submission to God there can be no holiness. When we refuse to submit to God, we are rejecting the Lordship of God over our life, and as such begin to doubt God's wisdom, become dismissive of His love, and begin to despise, scorn and disdain the Word.

Seeing the consequences of not submitting to God, the question that arises is how do we acquire the discipline of submission?

The simple answer to this all important question is by knowing our General, knowing His nature, knowing His character, knowing His faithfulness, knowing His omnipotence, and trusting Him to lead us to victory in all things.

In his letter to Timothy, Paul encourages him to adopt a certain mindset concerning ministry that can also be brought into the discussion of learning to submit to God.

2 Timothy 2:3, "You therefore must endure hardship as a good soldier of Jesus Christ."

The first thing a newly enlisted soldier learns, before he gets to play with guns and learn tactics, is submitting to authority. The entire success of a military operation hinges on whether or not the soldier submits to the authority of his commanding officer, and obeys the commands that are given to him.

In the country of my birth enlisting in the armed forces was mandatory. Every male would have to enlist for no less than eighteen months after they turned eighteen, and although my family was kicked out of the country before I came of age – we were deported because my grandfather was a Bible smuggler, but that's a story for another time – I heard the stories my father and grandfather told of their time in the armed forces. They both agreed that the hardest part for them was learning to submit to the authority of their superior officer without delay and without objection. They had to learn to discipline themselves into submitting. They had to discipline themselves into not raising any objections.

Imagine an army on the battlefield facing down its sworn enemy, and as the commanding officer gives the order to engage, all the enlisted men of his platoon start offering their opinion on the matter.

"With all due respect sir, I don't think that's a very good idea. Instead of engaging the enemy, why not retreat to higher ground?"

"Your plan is sound sir, no offense intended, but I think I've come up with a better way. In my honest opinion I think we should try to talk the enemy into surrendering rather than actively engaging them in battle."

It would be utter chaos. Confusion would sweep the ranks, no one would know what to do, and that moment of inaction, that moment of being trapped in indecision will have been enough for the enemy to gain the upper hand, to advance, and to overtake your position.

Then there are those who just enlisted for the signing bonus whatever they thought that bonus would be. Whether prosperity, good health or straight teeth, such individuals enlisted not to defend truth, but to receive some benefit for having enlisted. These are individuals who would rather just surrender to the enemy than have to exert themselves in combat.

Whether we want to admit it to ourselves or not, the churches today are packed to the rafters with individuals who enlisted simply because they were promised something tangible and material in return. Theirs is not the way of a true soldier, but rather it is the way of a profiteer, a mercenary, someone who will switch sides in a heartbeat if the offer on the table was substantive enough.

Because many believers today are not fully invested, because they believe in their hearts that compromise and duplicity are acceptable in the sight of God, we have a generation of supposed soldiers who are averse to both confrontation and battle. Such individuals spend more time second guessing God and His commands than they do actively confronting the darkness.

The examples are limitless, but the end result of this exercise is always the same. When the soldier does not obey his commanding officer's orders, there is a breakdown in the cohesion of the unit, and the objective is never reached.

Our General is far better equipped in both knowledge and experience confronting the enemy than we are. He knows the enemy's tactics, the means by which he attacks, and in His goodness He commands us, that we might be victorious in the battle. If we choose to disregard His orders, it will be to our detriment, because without obedience, without submission, all our struggle is in vain.

Paul encourages Timothy to be a good soldier, even a single-minded soldier of Jesus Christ. If Jesus commands me to be righteous, then I do not question His orders, I submit to His authority and carry out my assignment.

It is common knowledge that an enlisted soldier can face a court martial for disobeying a direct order from a superior officer. If the standard of the world is set at such a high level, what makes us think God's standard is lower?

We must realize that God knows the enemy better than we can ever hope to know him. As such we must trust in the wisdom of our General, and submit to His authority that we might win the battle, and obtain the victory.

God knows that our enemy will not be talked down. He knows that our enemy cannot be reasoned with, because he is as a roaring lion, the madness of his rage knowing no limits, and the sum of all his energies are directing at destroying the children of God.

The devil knows he can't hurt God directly, so he attempts to break God's heart indirectly by going after His children. Jesus is a good general, and as any good general will tell you, he feels the loss of those under his command deeply and profoundly.

If we are good soldiers of Jesus Christ, then we must submit to His authority. We have enlisted, and we are at war. Make no mistake about it, every day of our lives we fight and we wrestle against principalities and powers, against the rulers of the darkness of this age, and against spiritual hosts of wickedness in the heavenly places. If we hope to win the battle, we must know the weapons of our warfare, and follow the orders of our General who is always before us.

With that protracted and meandering introduction out of the way let us circle back to the preeminent question of this chapter, and answer it as truthfully as possible: Do you know your General?

The question isn't whether you know of Him, the question isn't whether others have told you about Him, the question isn't even if you read about Him in the Bible, or listened to sermons as to who He is. The question is, do you know Him.

Do you know God personally and intimately? Is He your God, or the God of your fathers? Is He your God or the God of your denomination?

Do you know your General? A simple enough question, but once we begin to delve deeper into this all important question, once we begin to peel back the layers, we come to understand that we must know God as He presents Himself to us, and not as others attempt to repackage Him.

If we do not know the true God, if we do not know God as He is meant to be known, then we know not His voice, and if we know not his voice, then anyone pretending to be Him will likely lead us astray.

Although some people claim to know who their General is, although they claim to know His many attributes, their failure to obey Him betrays the fact that they don't truly know Him.

As far as leaders go there are those who lead from afar, or from the rear as modern day parlance is fond of saying, and those who lead from the front. There are leaders who give orders without thought or consequence for their soldiers, then there are leaders who respect their men to such an extent that they do their utmost to keep from losing even a one.

We serve a God who leads from the front. No matter how fearsome the battle, no matter how vast the enemy hordes, you will always find your General where the battle is thickest, where the battle is at its most brutal, and you will find him perpetually protecting and defending His soldiers.

It is said that if you want to know the truth about a commanding officer you need look no further than the men under his command. What they have to say about him will likely shed as much light as any resume, and whether for the good or for the bad, men under someone's command know the character of the individual almost immediately.

In order to truly know your General, it is a worthwhile endeavor to look back at what some of the most notable warriors in the history of the world had to say about Him.

Unlike Moses who was prophet of God, Joshua was all warrior. Joshua was Moses's second in command until Moses died, and is considered one of the Bible's greatest military leaders. Although Joshua had supernatural experiences with God in his own right, he is best known for his military ingenuity, rather than his communing with God has Moses had. It was Joshua who led the seven-year campaign to conquer the promised land, something he was ultimately successful in.

Joshua knew battle, he knew war, he knew tactics and had an enviable militarily strategic mind, but he also trusted in the arm of the Lord, and every time he placed his trust in the Lord he was never disappointed.

It was at the tail end of his life, after he had fought battles, and conquered lands, and saw the hand of God present every step of the way that Joshua makes this assessment of his General:

Joshua 24:14-15, "Now therefore, fear the Lord, serve Him in sincerity and in truth, and put away the gods which your fathers served on the other side of the River and in Egypt. Serve the Lord! And if it seems evil to you to serve the Lord, choose for yourselves this day whom you will serve, whether the gods which your fathers served that were on the other side of the River, or the gods of the Amorites, in whose land you dwell. But as for me and my house, we will serve the Lord."

Although there are many nuggets of wisdom to mine in just these two verses, the salient, overarching point as far as the context of this train of thought is concerned, is that Joshua spoke these words not at the beginning of a long and distinguished career as a warrior in God's army, but at the end of his life.

After every battle had been fought, after every victory had been won, after seeing all that he saw, Joshua's assessment was that he along with his household would continue to serve the Lord.

We are all young and impressionable once. There are people who fall for Scientology nowadays, so we know that whether rich or poor, famous or unknown, at a certain point in our lives we all get duped a little now and again.

The older we get, however, the wiser we get, and based on previous experiences we are less likely to be fooled, less likely to fall for the fanciful promises of impotent gods, and more likely to judge rightly as opposed to when we were younger.

Joshua had no reputation to protect or maintain. He was dying, and he knew it. His reputation as one of the greatest figures in Israel's history was already cemented, and if his General had ever failed him, if he had ever felt let down by God, he would not have made the declaration that he made regarding Him.

Not only did Joshua purpose to serve the Lord based on the amalgam of experiences he'd had with Him throughout his long and storied life, he also pledged the allegiance of his family.

Even the most heartless among us wouldn't drag his wife, his children, his grandchildren and all his blood relatives into a lie knowingly, and willingly. If there was any lingering doubt in Joshua's heart as to the character of his general, if there was even an ounce of inconsistency in His faithfulness, Joshua may have pledged his own allegiance, but would have likely left his family out of the fray.

Another great soldier who saw the consistent faithfulness of his General and was able to articulate it brilliantly was King David. Yes, David started out as a shepherd boy, but even as a shepherd boy he knew that if he placed his trust in God, God would never let him down or disappoint him.

One of the greatest lessons we can learn from David's life is to believe God for big things, and believe that He will come through. David's life taught us to build upon our faith, and grow in our faith with every victory God provides, with every battle we see His hand in, with every vanquishing of the enemy in our life.

Given extensive research and some deductive reasoning, David could not have been more than 15 years of age when he confronted Goliath. Some scholars stipulate that he could have been as young as 12, but even 15 seems like someone awfully young to stand against a man whose coat of mail alone weighed around 125 pounds.

David had no training in the art of war, he did not know how to wield a sword or raise a shield, but what he did have was the certainty of victory based on past experiences.

He had already killed both a lion and a bear who had come to take lambs out of his father's flock. He had already seen the hand of God, and he knew what his General was capable of.

David knew two very important things. First, David knew where he ended and God began. He knew that it was the Lord who delivered him form the paw of the lion and from the paw of the bear. Second, David knew that if God could deliver him from both lion and bear, he would surely deliver him from the hand of the Philistine.

1 Samuel 17:36-37, "Your servant has killed both lion and bear; and this uncircumcised Philistine will be like one of them, seeing he has defied the armies of the living God.' Moreover David said, 'The Lord, who delivered me from the paw of the lion and form the paw of the bear, He will deliver me from the hand of the Philistine.' And Saul said to David, 'Go and the Lord be with you.'"

We all know how the story ends. We know that David felled Goliath and cut off his head with Goliath's own sword. We likewise know that whatever ups and downs David might have had, his faith in his General never once faltered. Throughout his life David remained as certain of God's ability to deliver him as he had been the day he stood against Goliath.

If we were to include all of David's words on God's ability to deliver, and His faithfulness throughout, we would have to include at least half of the Psalms and a quarter of the second book of Samuel. David was a most prolific writer of the Old Testament when it came to testifying of God's goodness, faithfulness, providence, omnipotence, and yes, even justice.

As such, I have selected a handful of verses from David's writings, and I have strived to include those he wrote towards the end of his life rather than at the beginning, the reason being that when speaking, or writing in hindsight, looking back over the years, an individual's assessment is most forthright and true.

It is both difficult and challenging to pick just a few verses that encompass all of David's praises of his General, and the fact that He saved him from so many enemies. Yet, one of the most fulfilling and illuminating things we can do as believers, is chronicle all the psalms and songs of thanksgiving David wrote regarding God's ever present faithfulness.

2 Samuel 22:1-4, "Then David spoke to the Lord the words of this song, on the day when the Lord had delivered him from the hand of all his enemies, and from the hand of Saul. And he said: 'The Lord is my rock, my fortress, and my deliverer; the God of my strength, in Him I will trust, my shield and the horn of my salvation, my stronghold and my refuge; my Savior, You save me from violence. I will call upon the Lord who is worthy to be praised; so shall I be saved from my enemies.'"

2 Samuel 22:29-40, "For You are my lamp, O Lord; the Lord shall enlighten my darkness. For by You I can run against a troop; by my God I can leap over a wall. As for God, His way is perfect; the word of the Lord is proven; He is a shield to all who trust in Him. For who is God, except the Lord? And who is a rock, except our God? God is my strength and power, and He makes my way perfect. He makes my feet like the feet of a deer, and sets me on my high places. He teaches my hands to make war, so that my arms can bend a bow of bronze. You have also given me the shield of your salvation, and Your gentleness has made me great. You enlarged my path under me; so my feet did not slip. I have pursued my enemies and destroyed them; neither did I turn back again till they were destroyed. And I have destroyed them and wounded them, so they could not rise; they have fallen under my feet. For you have armed me with strength for the battle; You have subdued under me those who rose against me.'"

Does this sound like a man who had any doubts as to God's ability to bring him through any circumstance victoriously? Does this sound like a man who had any doubts as to his General's character and love for His troops? Does this sound like a man who had any doubts as to God's omnipotence and absolute control over any situation?

David wrote this song on the day the Lord delivered him from the hand of *all* his enemies. He wrote this song when all his battles had been fought, when all his wars had been won, and when throughout all of it God had proven Himself without a shadow of turning.

This was, in essence, his assessment of God's presence in his life, the assessment of his General's presence on the battlefield, and his conclusion that without God by his side, without God actively providing the victory he would have been long dead, a sad footnote in the history of Israel.

2 Samuel 22:47-51, "The Lord Lives! Blessed be my Rock! Let God be exalted, the Rock of my salvation! It is God who avenges me, who subdues the people under me, who delivers me from my enemies. You also lift me above those who rise against me; you have delivered me from the violent man. Therefore, I will give thanks to You, o Lord, among the Gentiles, and sing praises to Your name. He is the tower of salvation to His king, and shows mercy to His anointed, to David and his descendants forevermore."

Depending on how one defines battle, David fought between twenty to sixty wars, battles, and skirmishes throughout his life. The reason the number varies so wildly depends on one's definition of what a battle is. If you include all the times Saul tried to have David killed, then the number grows exponentially. If you include only the battles David fought against other nations and tribes, then the number settles at around twenty.

Even at twenty, the number is impressive. How many people do you know that have fought twenty wars? I once met a man who somehow managed to fight in the second world war, the Korean war, and Vietnam, but individuals who've seen more than three wars throughout their life, especially nowadays, are few and far in between.

Imagine twenty wars. Imagine twenty different fighting styles, twenty different military strengths, some armies favoring horses, others chariots, others swords, others bows, other spears. Imagine having to strap on your armor every time, take to the battlefield, oftentimes outnumbered, and do so with the absolute certainty that God would provide you with victory. Even when you couldn't see it, even when the numbers were stacked against you, even when your enemy had outflanked you, still fighting on, knowing that somehow your General would come through.

Do you know your General? This is a fundamental question, and it goes beyond a yes or no answer. The question isn't so much if you know your General, but do you know Him as He is, or as some watered down, weakened, absentee commander who would never step foot on the battlefield, or raise a sword against the enemy?

Do you know Him as some disengaged deity looking down from heaven hoping you succeed but never really doing anything to help, or do you know Him as an active, engaged, present God who stands with you on the day of battle, and fights on your behalf?

Anyone who has ever put on the whole armor of God and has stood on the battlefield knows the reality of knowing God stands with them. Anyone who has stood their ground against the darkness, who placed truth above all else, who trumpeted Jesus even at the sake of their very lives, knows the reality of the words David spoke.

It is God who is our rock, it is God who is our shield, it is God who is our light, and it is God who is our strength. He has proven faithful throughout, and though I have met many now in the twilight of their life who have served God for decades, I've never met anyone who has put their trust in Him only to see Him fail them.

The list does not begin and end with Joshua and David. Throughout the Word of God, both in the Old and New Testament we see declaration upon declaration regarding our General's faithfulness from Elijah, to Elisha, to Jeremiah, to Ezekiel, to Nahum, to Obadiah, to Paul, to Peter, to John, and the rest of the great men of the Bible.

Although some skeptic somewhere might say that the experiences of these men are anecdotal, the pattern paints a portrait even the most hardened skeptic cannot deny.

One out of three might be anecdotal, ten out of a hundred might be anecdotal, but when every single individual who formed a bond and relationship with their General only spoke of His greatness, faithfulness, and ability to defy odds when it came to defeating the enemy, the evidence speaks for itself.

One of the must humbling things we can discover about our General is His authentic and perpetual desire to have a relationship with all of His soldiers. It matters not where you are stationed, it matters not what your rank is in His army, from the lowliest cook, to the mightiest of commanders, God's desire is intimacy and relationship.

Only by developing these virtues, only by having a relationship with our General can we discern his voice, and obey His commands without hesitation.

How can anyone claim to belong to the army of God when they never knew the true God? How can anyone claim to serve at the behest of the God of the Bible when the god they worship is a construct of their own making, an all permissive, impotent, man-like god who has no expectations or places any requirements on those who serve him?

The only individuals who have ever claimed that God has failed them were individuals who were worshiping gods of their own design, then expected the one true God to get them out of trouble when they found themselves in a pinch.

God has no obligation toward those who are not His!

Lest we forget the Bible does speak of illegitimate children, it speaks of men and women who give themselves honorary titles of sons and daughters of God, but whom God never knew.

In order for God to know us, we must strive to know God. We must strive for intimacy and fellowship with Him not because we can get something from Him but for the sake of the intimacy and fellowship itself.

We live in an age wherein many a churchgoer has a vested interest when it comes to spending time with God. We have been taught this from our pulpits, it's blaring at us from our television sets, and more and more individuals have come to believe that if you can fake it long enough God will send you a million dollar check in the mail.

That is not intimacy, and that's not what God is looking for. Far too often those who ought to know Him best treat God as a dementia ridden aunt who has a bunch of money, and who we take out for pudding and ice cream once in a while hoping she leaves us some of the loot in her will.

We fail to grasp the incomparable beauty of the fact that we are inheriting a Kingdom, a Kingdom which the Son of God Himself went to prepare for us.

Let's face it, if most supposed Christians knew their General, if most supposed Christians really knew the one true God, then they would be able to describe Him in a much more comprehensive manner.

If someone were to ask you if you knew me, and you said, "yeah, I know him, he's that dark fellow with the lazy eye and the peg leg", then by that very description you would have betrayed the fact that you don't really know me.

If when asked about who God is, most believers describe Him as some daddy big bucks up in heaven who needs to be entertained in order to throw a few shekels our way, or as some all permissive deity who laughs at our sin and our trampling upon the blood of His own Son, then by our very definition of Him we betray the fact that we don't really know Him.

If the God you serve does not fall within the parameters of the God of the Bible, then you are not serving the God of the Bible. If you are not serving the God of the Bible, then expect whichever god you serve to be your present help in time of trouble, but not the one true God.

We cannot redefine God without consequence. We cannot cherry pick the attributes we like about Him and throw the rest away and still presume to be serving Him. It doesn't work that way. Everyone who has thought themselves wiser than God discovered that they were not. Everyone who has presumed to pull one over on God for some earthly gain or another, belatedly realized that God knows the heart, He know the intent of the heart, and there is no fooling Him.

How do we know if we are worshipping the one true God? How do we know if the voice we are hearing is the voice of our General and not some imposter? By going to His Word and allowing it to paint a portrait of who our God is.

If the image you have of God clashes with how the Word describes Him, then know that it is you who are wrong and not the Bible. It is we who must bend and acquiesce to the will and word of the Father, not the other way around.

In recent years there has been a new crop of heresy making the rounds within the church, insisting that what God wants is not obedience, but a conversation. Whenever you hear the words 'God wants to have a conversation', that's code for *'we're going to try and change God's mind on something that is explicit within His Word.'*

This sort of nonsense is usually spouted by twenty something bespectacled hipsters who have no eyesight problems, but believe that by wearing horn rimmed glasses it gives them an air of intellectual gravitas.

As appealing as the idea of God wanting my input on how He runs the universe might be, the prospect itself is foolishness on its face, and what's more, it goes against Scripture itself.

God doesn't want my input; He wants my obedience. God doesn't want my opinion; He wants my devotion. God doesn't want my trinkets and baubles; He wants my heart.

So who is our General as the Bible describes Him? Who is our God as His own Word defines Him to be? Although you might be tempted to gloss over the following Bible passages, I urge and beseech you not to, because contained therein is not only the character and nature of our General, but the standard to which He expects His soldiers to live up to.

Exodus 34:5-7, "Then the Lord descended in the cloud and stood with him there, and proclaimed the name of the Lord. And the Lord passed before him and proclaimed, "the Lord, the Lord God, merciful and gracious, longsuffering, and abounding in goodness and truth, keeping mercy for thousands, forgiving iniquity and transgression and sin by no means clearing the guilty, visiting the iniquity of the fathers upon the children and the children's children to the third and fourth generation."

We see one of the first glimpses of the nature of God, and it is a balanced one. He is merciful and gracious, longsuffering, and abounding in goodness and truth, but by the same token he will not acquit the guilty. Even as early as the book of Exodus God Himself annihilates the notion of universalism, or the belief that God will overlook our iniquities even if they are not repented of.

Numbers 23:19, "God is not a man, that He should lie, nor a son of man, that He should repent. Has He said, and will He not do it or has He spoken, and will He not make it good?"

Herein we have another glimpse into the nature of God, another virtue He possess, and that is steadfastness. If God says a thing, He will do it, for if He says a thing not only is it within His power to perform it, but He will let nothing stand in the way of Him fulfilling His promise. God is consistent, God is faithful, and God is steadfast. It is we who waver and doubt, it is we who second guess and question, for if we stood on His promises knowing He will keep them, then there would be no circumstance or scenario through which we could not pass joyfully.

Deuteronomy 4:24, "For the Lord your God is a consuming fire, a jealous God."

Deuteronomy 10:17, "For the Lord your God is God of gods and Lord of lords, the great God, mighty and awesome, who shows no partiality nor takes a bribe."

Deuteronomy 20:4, "For the Lord your God is He who goes with you, to fight for you against your enemies, to save you."

Deuteronomy 33:27, "The eternal God is your refuge, and underneath are the everlasting arms; He will thrust out the enemy from before you, and will say, 'Destroy!'"

Other than the book of Psalms, the book of Deuteronomy has some of the most telling and explicit descriptions as to the nature of God, and His position in relation to those who serve and obey Him.

As previously stated, God is neither indifferent, disengaged, nor absentee. God is present, engaged, and it is He who goes with us, to fight against our enemies, and to save us. Our God is both mighty and awesome, jealous and impartial. He is the God of gods and the Lord of lords, and He stands at the head of His army ready to do battle on our behalf.

> *Psalm 33:11-23, "The counsel of the Lord stands forever, the plans of His heart to all generations. Blessed is the nation whose God is the Lord, and the people whom He has chosen as His own inheritance. The Lord looks from heaven; He sees all the sons of men. From the place of His habitation He looks on all the inhabitants of the earth; He fashions their hearts individually; He considers all their works. No king is saved by the multitude of an army; a mighty man is not delivered by great strength. A horse is a vain hope for safety; neither shall it deliver any by its great strength. Behold, the eye of the Lord is on those who fear Him, on those who hope in His mercy, to deliver their soul from death, and to keep them alive in famine. Our soul waits for the Lord; He is our help and our shield. For our heart shall rejoice in Him, because we have trusted in His holy name. Let Your mercy, O Lord, be upon us, just as we hope in You."*

> *Psalm 48:14, "For this is God, our God forever and ever; He will be our guide even to death."*

> *Psalm 50:6, "Let the heavens declare His righteousness for God Himself is Judge. Selah"*

Psalm 68:19-20, "Blessed be the Lord, who daily loads us with benefits, the God of our salvation! Selah Our God is the God of salvation; and to God the Lord belongs escapes from death."

Psalm 84:11-12, "For the Lord God is a sun and shield; the Lord will give grace and glory; no good thing will He withhold from those who walk uprightly. O Lord of hosts, blessed is the man who trusts in You!"

Psalm 116:5, "Gracious is the Lord, and righteous; Yes, our God is merciful."

If one's desire is to understand the multifaceted nature of God, and see Him for who He is, there is no better place to begin one's journey than the book of Psalms. The psalms were written by men who experienced the saving power of God firsthand, who saw His restorative, forgiving, merciful hand at work in their own lives, and who were in awe of His righteousness.

These are not second hand accounts or the musings of some stale, aging academic whose credentials exceed his intelligence. These are not hypothetical ruminations brought upon by a desire to manufacture a new way of seeing God, when the old way had sufficed for thousands of years.

These are firsthand accounts of God's presence and glory, firsthand accounts of seeing victory snatched out of the hands of defeat, of seeing lives supernaturally preserved contrary to prevailing circumstances.

When the men who penned the Psalms, and yes, more than David's psalms are included in the book of Psalms, they did it from a place of worship, and thankfulness, and gratitude, and love for God. Their discourses on God are not dry and cold. These men lived what they penned, the witnessed the things they testified about, and their writings are steeped in passion, because to know God, to truly know God, is to love, worship, and serve Him passionately.

I for one cannot reconcile the notion of casual Christianity with the knowledge of God. If I truly know God, then the notion of serving Him casually goes out the window. If I truly know God, then I can never be satisfied with two hours twice a week in His presence, but will desire to bask in His glory in perpetuity.

I fear that many believers today are not passionate about God because they do not know the one true God. They do not know the God of Abraham, Isaac, and Jacob, they do not know the God of the Bible, they know a tamed, restrained, subdued, and almost subjugated version of God.

They know the inoffensive god of the modern age, a god very different from the one true God the Bible depicts and speaks of. There is a balance to the God of the Bible, an amalgam of mercy and righteousness, love and judgment, gentleness and strength. If we only attribute certain ones of His attributes to Him, then we make God less than what He is thereby creating our own version of a God.

If you were to prepare a dish but left out half the ingredients, would the dish be the same as it would have been with all the ingredients?

If you were to take a car apart and only put half the pieces back together would it still resemble a car, and if so, would it still run and perform as it would have if it had all its parts?

This is why it is of utmost importance for us to know the God of the Bible as He presents Himself in His word and not some man-made variation of Him.

Since we've seen glimpses of God's character and nature throughout the Old Testament, and these were by no means comprehensive as far as including all the passages, I want to go through a few of the passages in the New Testament regarding God so the reality that God changes not crystalizes in our minds and hearts.

The Old and the New Testament do not present two different versions of God. They do not present two different versions of our General. They are as one, the latter being a continuation of the former.

The one difference between the Old and New Testaments, is the manifestation of God's love in the flesh, His son Jesus, our Lord, the mechanism by which man might be reconciled unto God. Yes, it is a big difference, it is the greatest of differences, but it does not change the nature of God, for He remained as He always was.

John 3:16, "For God so loved the world that He gave His only begotten Son, that whoever believes in Him should not perish but have everlasting life."

Herein we see the extent of God's love for the world He created in that He gave His only begotten Son, so those who believe in Him might have everlasting life. This is God's proven love, not God's theoretical love. There is no more that God can do to prove that He loves you and me than what He has already done.

Romans 11:22, "Therefore consider the goodness and severity of God: on those who fell, severity; but toward you, goodness, if you continue in His goodness. Otherwise you also will be cut off."

Again we see the balance of the God we serve, and it is beautifully illustrated in Paul's letter to the Romans. Paul warns that we must consider both the goodness and the severity of God. To dismiss one or the other is to be flawed in our approach of Him. When we contemplate only the goodness of God, we fail to truly grasp the dangers of transgressing, and of not continuing in His goodness. When we consider only the severity of God we are perpetually looking over our shoulder, beaten and downtrodden, half expecting the rod of God to smite us at any moment.

Consider the goodness and severity of God, for He is goodness, and shows goodness toward those who love Him, but He also shows severity toward those who fell and did not repent. Only when we consider both do we get a complete portrait of who God is.

1 Corinthians 1:9, "God is faithful, by whom you were called into the fellowship of His Son, Jesus Christ our Lord."

1 Corinthians 4:20, "For the kingdom of God is not in word but in power."

Galatians 6:7-8, "Do not be deceived, God is not mocked; for whatever a man sows, that he will also reap. For he who sows to his flesh will of the flesh reap corruption, but he who sows to the Spirit will of the Spirit reap everlasting life."

1 John 1:5-7, "This is the message which we have heard from Him and declare to you, that God is light and in Him is no darkness at all. If we say that we have fellowship with Him, and walk in darkness, we lie and do not practice the truth. But if we walk in the light as He is in the light, we have fellowship with one another, and the blood of Jesus Christ His Son cleanses us from all sin."

Revelation 21:3, "And I heard a loud voice from heaven saying, 'Behold the tabernacle of God is with men, and He will dwell with them, and they shall be His people, and God Himself will be with them and be their God."

From Genesis through to the book of Revelation, we see the continuity of God's character and nature. God never stops being merciful and loving, but He never stops being just and righteous either. God never stops being a strong tower to those who love Him, but He never stops punishing the unrighteous.

Those who believe that God has changed are simply projecting their own temporal desires on an eternal God. They are speaking their hopes of a changing God rather than the reality of an unchanging one because they know deep in their souls that their lives are not in harmony with Him and His will for their lives.

When a soul realizes it is not in harmony with its Creator, when it realizes that it has wandered beyond His arm of protection and grace, the only two options it is left with is to either return with repentance to the foot of the cross, or attempt to transform the very nature of God to suit their compromises.

Which path they choose, which option they choose to exercise depends wholly on whether they love their sin more than they love God, or if they love God more than they love their sin. There is only room for one on the throne of every heart. The Word is explicit when it informs us that we cannot serve two masters, so whether we want to admit it or not, we will always love one more than the other, whether it's God or the world.

Do we live to serve Him or do we live to serve the self? Do we live to obey Him without question or do we seek to undermine His authority at every turn? Although the preceding assertions might seem anathema to some, even taking offense at the prospect of attempting to undermine God or serve self rather than Him, it is nevertheless something the modern day church has had to wrestle with more frequently than one might think.

Whenever man's opinion trumps the Word of God, whenever the will of man supersedes God's commands, whenever men choose to accept doctrine that tickles their ears rather than convicts them of their sin, they are in essence undermining the authority of God Himself.

His Word tells us that God is faithful, God is light, God is power, God is truth, God is justice. His Word reveals our General's character more thoroughly than the words of any man, and if in our hearts and minds we have another image of who God is, it is an image we've concocted in and of ourselves without any foundation or undergirding of truth.

Do you know your General? Do you know Him as others who came before you did? Do you know Him as faithful and true, as one who leads the charge against the darkness and doesn't merely sit on the sidelines giving orders? If so, then there ought to be no compunction about following Him wherever He leads, about obeying every command that He gives, and about standing your ground even when it seems you are outnumbered and the chances of survival are slim to none.

Our General does not make mistakes. Our General will not send us into battle without a clear path to victory. Our General will not risk His soldiers for vainglory or to make a point. He is a good General, one who cares for His troops, and one who has ensured them victory if they trust and obey Him to the end.

CHAPTER NINE

DO YOU KNOW YOURSELF?

If we call ourselves children of God we are already at war. I want to keep hammering home this point, so that we might better understand the seriousness of the season we are living in. The enemy does have a plan, he is tactically literate, and he knows our vulnerabilities. A wise man, a battle-ready believer likewise knows himself, knows his strengths, his attributes and his gifting, but also knows his weaknesses and guards against them most fiercely.

Brutal honesty is the prerequisite to knowing oneself. If I am unwilling to be honest about my heart, my spiritual condition, my temperament, my predilections, my predispositions and my weaknesses I will never truly know myself but only the version of myself that I want to see staring back at me in the mirror.

We as a species like to project. We like to see the best possible version of ourselves in ourselves rather than the reality that is. As such, whole cottage industries have sprung up wherein their only spiel is making you feel good about the current you, without the need to peel back the façade of your projection and begin to make the requisite changes.

Nowadays honesty has been redefined to the point that if you insist on being completely honest with someone, chances are you'll be accused of bullying or some sort of bigotry. My being honest with you about your spiritual condition and pointing you to the Word of God for the remedy thereof does not constitute bullying or bigotry; it is love.

Self-assessment is mandatory for every child of God, and if after you've assessed yourself you conclude that you have no weaknesses, no chinks in your armor, no pressure points the enemy can exploit, then you either didn't look hard enough, or were not honest with yourself. All of us have weaknesses. All of us have points wherein if enough pressure is applied we will wince and react.

Your weakness, whatever that might be, is the device the enemy most often employs to try to derail you and vanquish you spiritually. Knowing the fact that the enemy employs your weakness against you, and knowing yourself well enough to know your own weakness, you are especially sensitive to any situation or circumstance in which this weakness can be exploited.

If alcohol is your weakness, then perhaps bars are not the best place for you to hang out. If lust is your weakness, then perhaps watching movies with innuendo and gratuitous nudity in them is not the best way to pass your time. You know your weakness! Guard against it and one of the enemy's greatest weapons against you will have been neutralized.

As Paul so poetically puts it, we ought to be aware of the devil's devices lest he get an advantage, or outwit us. Paul understood the battle and what it meant. He knew that it was not a battle for something as fleeting as statehood or nationality, but for one's eternal soul and where it would spend eternity. Throughout the New Testament we are warned to be on guard, to be alert, to watch, to be aware, to prepare, to put on our armor, because the ramifications of this war we wage are greater than the ramifications of any physical war.

Not only does not knowing yourself endanger you personally, it also endangers those you go into battle with, those you call your brothers and sisters in arms. Although you might be able to mask your weakness when no pressure is brought to bear, if it is not dealt with, if it is not shored up, if you have not done everything that was in your power to do to guard against it, in the heat of battle your weakness will manifest and become visible, like an ink stain on a white sheet.

Because *'leave no man behind'* is not only the warrior's ethos it is the Christian's ethos as well, by not being diligent in guarding against what you knew was a likely point of ingress for the enemy, you have essentially endangered your entire unit by your carelessness.

We are brothers. We feel for each other as only those who have seen battle together can, and so if my brother or sister is hobbled or slowed down, my instinct is to go help them, to give them a shoulder to lean on, and hopefully make it to safety together.

The enemy poses enough of a danger without us giving him an advantage. The enemy is wily enough on his own without us making it easier for him to fell us by having hidden sin in our lives, or living in a duplicitous and hypocritical manner.

We have seen far too many examples of men whose weaknesses the devil exploited for his benefit in recent years, and without fail there has always been collateral damage. It's not just a pastor or an evangelist that falls when they get exposed for living in sin, it is large swaths of individuals who looked up to these men as well.

I could name names, and there would be a substantial list of those who were felled in battle because of their unguarded weaknesses, but what would be the point? I'm certain you've already thought of a couple names yourself.

Your weakness doesn't necessarily have to be a sin; it can also be a consistent practice that keeps you from fulfilling your calling in some form or measure. It was some years ago that I realized the weakness the enemy loved to exploit in my life on a consistent basis was my propensity for procrastination.

I am the worst procrastinator on the planet. If I sit down to do something and there is any possibility of being distracted, even a miniscule one, chances are better than good the enemy will bring it to the forefront and tempt me with it.

Because I was able to identify my weakness, I took steps to guard against it, and to some, the steps I took might be seen as nothing less than extreme. Whether others consider the measures you take in order to guard against your weakness extreme is irrelevant. You know what is necessary for you to guard against it, so you must do it even if others balk at the thought.

As far as my propensity for procrastination is concerned, I realized I could best guard against it by setting deadlines for myself. I knew myself well enough to know that I work best under pressure, and so if I had a deadline for a certain project I would work harder and longer to make sure it was finished.

I also took steps to eliminate distractions during the time I was working, or praying, or meditating on the Word, or whatever else I had set time aside for.

As such, when I sit down to write I unplug my router, and have no access to the internet, I shut off my phone, I close my office door, I sit in my chair, and I know I have two hours to either sit there and stare at the ceiling, or be productive.

When I set aside time for prayer, I go into my little nook, I close the door, I take my Bible, and allow no distractions to hinder me from spending time with God on that day.

Sometimes the hardest thing is breaking the habit, whatever the habit might be. It took me a good two weeks to get over the itchy finger syndrome when I sat down to write, because I would usually check out news sites, click on links that were e-mailed to me, go through my e-mails, and various other things that would just eat away the day. Without access to the internet doing these things became impossible, so to a certain extent I was forced to focus on the task at hand.

The Bible contains some of the most brutal and honest self-assessments ever to have been written, and they were done by men who are now looked upon as giants of the faith. These men were so honest and so self-aware, that even when angels of the Lord called them brave or righteous they corrected the messengers of the Lord, informing them to the contrary.

One of the most powerful self-assessments ever to have been recorded in the Bible is that of Isaiah. It is so poignant and there is so much to learn from Isaiah's reaction to seeing the Lord sitting on the throne, that it is worthwhile to pursue this avenue if only for the briefest of moments.

> *Isaiah 6:1-5, "In the year that King Uzziah died, I saw the Lord sitting on the throne, high and lifted up, and the train of His robe filled the temple. Above it stood seraphim; each one had six wings: with two he covered his face with two he covered his feet, with two he flew. And one cried to another and said "Holy, holy, holy, is the Lord of hosts; the whole earth is full of His glory!" And the posts of the door were shaken by the voice of him who cried out, and the house was filled with smoke. Then I said: "Woe is me, for I am undone! Because I am a man of unclean lips, and I dwell in the midst of a people of unclean lips; For my eyes have seen the King, the Lord of hosts."'*

Just for an instant I want you to consider how amazing Isaiah's response was upon seeing the vision that he saw. This was a man who was granted the honor and privilege of seeing the Lord sitting on the throne, of seeing the six winged seraphim, and of hearing them crying out to one another.

You can count the men who had a vision of God on His throne on one hand. Keep in mind this is over a four-thousand-year span of human history, so those are some pretty slim odds.

The only other men in the Bible to have explicitly seen the Lord on His throne were Micaiah, Ezekiel, Stephen, and John. There were others such as Moses who saw the back of God, or Jacob who dreamed of a ladder that reached to heaven and the Lord stood above it, or Paul who said he knew a man who was caught up to the third heaven, but as far as my research concludes, there were only five men including Isaiah who saw the Lord on His throne.

Imagine what the reaction of a man without self-awareness might have been upon having seen such an awe inspiring vision. I humbly submit that chances are better than good an overwhelming swath of Christendom today would conclude that they were worthy of seeing such a vision if they were shown such a vision, and so there was no need for them to acknowledge their flaws, shortcomings and weaknesses.

Isaiah was a man who knew himself. He knew himself well enough and was humble enough to acknowledge that he was a man of unclean lips dwelling in the midst of a people of unclean lips, and as such the conclusion he came to was that he was undone, destroyed, cut off.

I wonder how many of us would say that about ourselves today after having seen what Isaiah saw. I wonder how many believers today would have the strength of character not to highlight their attributes but to go straight to their shortcoming and be honest about it.

As long as our sin, shortcoming, or weakness remains a secret the enemy has the upper hand. As long as our sin, shortcoming, or weakness remains a secret the enemy has the tactical advantage, and at the most crucial moment he will use our weakness against us.

When we confess our sin as the Word instructs, the enemy no longer has power, nor does he have the upper hand. We have essentially shut down any avenue of attack our trespass may have opened up to him once we've confessed our sin and repented of it.

It is in our silence and obfuscation that we make ourselves of no effect in the battle, because we have been compromised by our unwillingness to unburden ourselves at the foot of the cross. A compromised individual knows that he is compromised, and in the hopes that the enemy will let him be does nothing that would make him a target or draw the enemy's ire.

Another Biblical author whose self-assessment is worthy of note is Paul the Apostle of Christ. Again, it is with brutal honesty and efficiency that he self-diagnoses himself, and points out the weaknesses he must contend with.

Once more, this is Paul we are talking about. The man whose first encounter with God was of the supernatural variety, having seen a light from heaven, and having heard the voice of Jesus. It was this man who became as ferocious a defender of truth as he had once been its enemy, and who suffered all things for the sake of Christ His Lord, that pens the following about himself.

Romans 7:15-24, "For what I am doing, I do not understand. For what I will to do, that I do not practice; but what I hate, that I do. If, then, I do what I will not to do, I agree with the law that it is good. But now, it is no longer I who do it, but sin that dwells in me. For I know that in me (that is, in my flesh) nothing good dwells; for to will is present with me, but how to perform what is good I do not find. For the good that I will to do, I do not do; but the evil I will not to do, that I practice. Now if I do what I will not to do, it is no longer I who do it, but sin that dwell sin mo. I find then a law, that evil is present with me, the one who wills to do good. For I delight in the law of God according to the inward man. But I see another law in my members, warring against the law of my mind, and bringing me into captivity to the law of sin which is in my members. O wretched man that I am! Who will deliver me from this body of death?"

Paul doesn't sweep anything under the rug, he doesn't justify anything, nor does he attempt to find excuses or ways of defending this ongoing struggle inside of himself. He acknowledges the struggle, he acknowledges the ongoing battle against the flesh, and he acknowledges the duality of every man wherein flesh and spirit collide and make war against each other.

It is only in the eighth chapter of Romans that Paul concludes his train of thought by declaring that only through Jesus are we made free of the law of sin, only by Him can we overcome.

Romans 8:5, "For those who live according to the flesh set their minds on the things of the flesh, but those who live according to the Spirit, the things of the Spirit. For to be carnally minded is death, but to be spiritually minded is life and peace."

It is we as individuals that must assess whether we are living in the flesh or living in the spirit. It is we as individuals who must be honest with ourselves and cry out to God for help in the areas which we are lacking.

Although there are different variations of the following truism, the essence of it is always the same. If you put two identical animals in a cage together, the animal that will survive, thrive, and eventually overcome the other is the one you feed.

If we feed the flesh, our minds will be set on the things of the flesh. If we feed the spiritual man, our minds will be set on spiritual things.

The accountability factor for us as believers and as soldiers of God is high. There is no place within the pages of Scripture that gives us license to shrug off personal accountability, nor is there any place in the Bible that insinuates we have a right to live as we please rather than in a manner that is pleasing to God.

As we read the words of those who came before us there are some who might assume that these men were simply self-deprecating. Personally, I believe that the closer we get to the light of God, the more vividly we see our own darkness and corruption. These men came very close to the source of all light, they came very close to the source of all truth, and as such they saw their true selves in contrast to God's perfection.

The more we see of our true selves in the light of God's righteousness, the more we will desire to be rid of the flesh, to shed it like an old skin and walk in His glorious grace.

Honesty is paramount when looking at ourselves in the mirror of God's word, doubly so because we know that the battle is upon us and we have to be fully equipped, shored up against our weaknesses, and ready to fight.

Not only are we repeatedly warned to prepare for battle, there are passages within God's Word which describe it, informing us that in the unseen realm, the whole of the universe is at war.

Revelation 12:7-8, "And war broke out in heaven: Michael and his angels fought against the dragon' and the dragon and his angels fought, but they did not prevail nor was a place found for them in heaven any longer."

Rovolation 13:7, "And it was granted to him to make war with the saints and to overcome them. And authority was given him over every tribe, tongue, and nation."

From what we read in God's Word there are three distinct groupings in this ongoing war. First, there is the army of heaven, the heavenly host, or the army of the Lord, second, there are the armies of darkness which include the devil, his angels, principalities, and powers, and third there is mankind, which is itself divided into two camps, the saints or the righteous, and the godless or unrighteous.

As I see it, every believer must choose one of two options: they can either learn how to properly use the weapons in their arsenal, shore up the lagging areas in their lives, learn what it is to do battle and spiritual warfare, or they can be fodder like so many clueless souls walking about vanquished, beaten, and imprisoned while ignorant of the fact they were at war to begin with.

It is because the household of faith has been infiltrated, and because we allowed the servants of darkness to teach that the war has been canceled and we are no longer in need of our weapons, that we now find ourselves outnumbered, with the enemy having successfully branched out and overtaken key positions.

We did not love the truth enough to defend it, we did not love the truth enough to fight for it, nor did we love the truth enough to lay our lives down as the Word tells us we ought, and we weren't honest enough with ourselves to acknowledge the need for God's help in our lives. We reveled in mediocrity, washed our hands in doubt, and clothed ourselves in indifference thinking ourselves spiritually superior for even contemplating the notion of God.

The half measure gospel has become the doctrine of the land, and the high priests of this gospel are reaping their rewards both in possessions, positions, and accolades from the world.

Just as not every citizen of a country is necessarily a soldier of the selfsame, sadly, not every Christian is a soldier in the army of God. But, make no mistake, there are still soldiers about.

Just as nations have traitors, so does the household of faith, but the difference between the nations and the church is that the nations prosecute their traitors while the church gives theirs a pass, citing the benefit of the doubt, because they just don't want the hassle, or Lord forbid to be thought of as intolerant or legalistic.

We are in the mess we are in because we looked the other way while sin ran amok, justified spiritually withered and dried individuals just because they looked good on camera, and came to believe that we could widen the path all on our own without any consequence or negative aftereffect.

We thought we could be what we wanted to be, live as we wanted to live, and demand that God embrace us as sons and daughters without hesitation.

The sad reality is that many individuals attempt to enlist in the army of God for the benefits, but very few want to put in the time and energy to go through the requisite training and learn what it really means to be a warrior for Christ, one whom the enemy identifies as a real and present threat, rather than some caricatures kicking a dummy around the altar talking about how they have the devil under their feet.

How can the enemy be under their feet if he is in their hearts? How can they sing of victory in Jesus when their entire spiritual life has been one long stretch of setbacks and defeat at the hands of the devil?

The enemy is more than happy to leave ignorant believers to their ignorance, because as long as he can keep them lethargic and sleeping, as long as he can distract them and keep them focused on other things, as long as he can keep them from pursuing godliness and righteousness, they will not be of any threat to him or his plans.

We no longer see our spiritual journey as a battle. We see it as a walk through the rose garden, replete with tweeting birds and flapping butterflies, because men have been telling us that's the way it's supposed to be for the better part of a decade.

We are told the comfort of the flesh and our individual happiness is paramount, and so that whole thing about obedience, sanctification, righteousness, and putting on our armor was for another time. All that talk about girding ourselves and readying for battle was for another season when men didn't have the internet and Facebook. Sure, those people had the time to learn the teachings of Christ, to walk in obedience to God's will, to live sanctified lives, because they didn't have cable and television.

We've got too much on our plate as is. Between the time we allot to frivolity, to the time we allot to useless endeavors, to the time we allot to daily labors, who has time for seeking the will of God anymore?

Do we realize how baseless our excuses for not doing as the Word of God commands us to do are? Do we realize that when we stand before God on that day of days we will have absolutely no excuse for the way we've prioritized our existence here on earth?

We cannot continue in this manner. It's that simple. If we think we can play with God, live lives of duplicity, and deem the devil harmless, we've got another thing coming, and when the bill comes due, when the reckoning becomes a present reality, there will be mourning and gnashing of teeth unlike the world has ever seen.

We can't blame it all on the devil. There, I said it. In fact, I'm going to say it again. We can't blame it all on the devil. The devil did what the devil does. He saw an opportunity, saw a chink in the armor, and saw a means by which to accelerate and achieve his plans and he took it.

It was your duty to make certain there was no chink in your armor. It was your duty to make certain you knew yourself well enough to know where the enemy was most likely to attack, and fortify that area of your life more than any other.

It is the watchman that stopped watching, the preacher that stopped preaching, the evangelist that stopped evangelizing, because, like little children they got distracted by the baubles and the shiny things, or concluded that they loved the world more than the truth so why not pursue it with abandon.

We lie to ourselves about ourselves with such regularity that we don't even believe the lies we tell ourselves anymore. Because we no longer believe the lies we tell ourselves we are on a constant search for validation and embrace anyone who is willing to validate us without pointing out the inconsistencies.

There is a futility in attempting to circumvent self-analysis in light of God's Word, because sooner or later it is you who will pay the price for failing to strengthen that which is weak, and make straight that which is crooked in your life.

Be self-aware at all times, and when you feel yourself drifting, when you feel the flesh attempting to mount an offensive, react quickly and decisively. Know your weakness and constantly guard against it, knowing it is your most vulnerable point, and as such the likeliest point of attack.

You know what your weakness is, and though no one else in your sphere of influence might, although they would never even guess at it, be assured that the enemy also knows it and is at this very moment devising his strategy against you.

Profound, protracted introspection of oneself is neither vain, wasteful, nor sinful if it is done in light of God's truth. There is only one truth, only one plumb line, only one yardstick by which we must measure ourselves, and it has nothing to do with subjectivity, our feelings, or how we think it ought to be.

The notion that you have your truth and I have my truth has become a popular heresy even within the church as of late, and each one, according to their own truth does as their truth dictates. As such, we have a church in disarray, each roaming about without any semblance of cohesion, without any semblance of unity, and without a clear and unifying directive.

That's the problem with forfeiting the truth of God for your own individual truth. When you prioritize your truth above God's truth you are no longer under His covering, you are no longer obeying His edicts, and you are no longer doing what you were commanded to do.

You are, in essence, a lone wolf going about your own self-appointed missions, living as you see fit, doing what seems right in your own eyes, and being accountable to no one but yourself. That may all be well and good until you find yourself outnumbered by the wolves and the vultures, alone, vulnerable, defenseless, with no supernatural arm to lean on, and no strong tower to run to.

Although many today are quick to widen the narrow path of faith and dynamite their way through every fundamental doctrine in the process, the truth remains that Christ is returning for a church without spot or wrinkle, and He will not compromise on this point.

It is up to us as individuals to look inward, to assess our hearts, and to determine whether there are any spots, wrinkles, or blemishes we must wash clean with the blood of the Lamb while we still have time, and while we are still able to do so.

Be honest about who you are, about your shortcomings, about your flaws, about your inconsistencies, about your inadequacies, and bring them all to the foot of the cross. Oftentimes honesty sounds like self-effacement but your concern ought not to be with what others think about you. Your singular concern ought to be what God thinks about you.

CHAPTER TEN

DO YOU KNOW YOUR ENEMY?

As followers of Christ we have an enemy. I realize this sounds simplistic, but if you've already acknowledged this all important truth, you are ahead of the game compared to many professing Christians today.

Some days I think we are living in an upside down world. We call ourselves Soldiers for Christ yet refuse to acknowledge we have an enemy, and that this enemy is anything but docile. We call ourselves warriors of truth yet refuse to acknowledge there is a battle that must be fought, there is an enemy that must be confronted, and there is energy that must be expelled.

Instead of acknowledging the existence of our enemy as well as his intent, we would rather pursue our *best lives now,* or endeavor to make *every day a Friday.* We have not the time for childish things any longer. We have not the time for distractions, we have not the time for foolishness, and we have not the time for believing teaching contrary to Scripture.

Not only is our enemy real, so are his agents and minions who have infiltrated the household of faith and wreak havoc with teachings that focus on this present life and all the baubles we can acquire, rather than the war that is raging in the spiritual realm, a war that has racked up a hefty body count of clueless believers.

The Word of God is clear and explicit as to the nature of our enemy, the intent of our enemy, and the prowess of our enemy. To underestimate the devil is to insure one's own demise, because no war has ever been won by underestimating one's foe.

How the household of faith can underestimate the cunning and prowess of a being that tried to overthrow God Himself and took 1/3 of the angels with him when he fell is beyond me. The devil is neither impotent nor is he powerless and to think otherwise is sheer folly.

Not only does the church presently underestimate the devil, it has somehow convinced itself that the devil doesn't really exist, and all the references to this mortal enemy of men's souls within the Bible are fictitious and parabolic teachings meant to deter men from wickedness rather than a real being.

As with so much nonsense being bandied about the household of faith nowadays, that's not what the Bible says!

If we cannot acknowledge the reality of the enemy we face, and accept that confrontation with said enemy is inevitable at some point in our life, then we will lose, and lose big.

Another thing we must always keep at the forefront of our minds whenever we engage the enemy is that he takes no prisoners. There has never been a more ruthless foe than the devil. The devil is not interested in a peace accord, he is not interested in a truce, he is not interested in a cease fire, and he is not interested in taking you prisoner only to exchange you for some of his own captured minions.

The devil cares not a whit for his followers, and so if they are felled, they are felled, and his thought runs to them nevermore. He has no reason, desire, or inclination to keep you alive, and so this struggle, this battle, this war, is always to the death.

Either you defeat the enemy and are crowned as an overcomer in the Kingdom, or you are defeated by the enemy and trod underfoot by him and his minions. There is no third option.

The life and death stakes of the battle must crystalize in the hearts and minds of all believers, so that every time they strap on their armor, every time they step onto the battlefield, they know that they are fighting for their very lives.

It is in the all or nothing mindset of their struggle that warriors are more apt to give it their all, to fight beyond the point of exhaustion, to fight beyond their fatigue, to press, and press, and press the enemy until he has been felled because the alternative is simply unacceptable.

We can wax poetic about the devil, but there is no poetry to him. He is a tireless, capable, ruthless, single minded machine that is constantly attempting to undermine, subvert, and delegitimize God and His Son Jesus, all the while attempting to tempt, deceive, and lead astray His followers.

The devil's motivation cannot be romanticized no matter how much the modern era attempts it, because his motivation is basic, naked, all-consuming hatred. There's no mystery there, there is no deeper meaning, all there is, is hatred for God, the things of God, and especially the followers of God.

The most succinct and defining portrayal of the enemy in the Bible comes from a very unlikely source. One would expect someone like Paul, or Luke to pen such definitive words, but it was left to a fisherman, someone of no notable grooming or education to get to the heart of the matter and warn the saints about the viciousness of the enemy they face.

1 Peter 5:8, "Be sober, be vigilant; because your adversary the devil walks about like a roaring lion seeking whom he may devour."

No long winded soliloquy, no in depth analysis as to the deeper motivations of the devil and whether or not he was right to be spurned because God showed more love toward His temporal creations, just the facts.

Within the span of one verse Peter identifies the adversary as well as his intent, warning those who would read his epistle to be sober and be vigilant.

You are soldier; be on guard. You are a soldier, be watchful. You are a soldier, be aware. You are a soldier, be awake. You are a soldier, be not distracted by the things of this world, or lulled to indifference by the siren's song of sloppy grace and bloodless conquests.

We have a duty to perform and it is to resist the devil, not try to understand him. Our calling is to fight the darkness not try to make peace with it, to do battle against principalities and powers, and not to roll over and play dead hoping they pass us by.

> 1 Peter 5:9, "Resist him, steadfast in the faith, knowing that the same sufferings are experienced by your brotherhood in the world."

There's a novel idea for the modern day church: resist the devil rather than appease him, resist the devil rather than placate him, resist the devil rather than try to understand him.

We're supposed to put up a fight. It's that simple! The fact that the church nowadays has lost the stomach for fighting the enemy only means they are in open rebellion against God and His Word. I realize it sounds harsh, but there's no way of sugarcoating this all important truth.

If we pose no threat to the enemy, if we do not mount a resistance against him, if all we are doing is gazing at our navels, plucking our nose hairs, and waiting for Jesus to appear in the sky, then we are doing something contrary and antithetical to what the Word of God commands us to do!

The devil hasn't stopped roaming, he hasn't stopped seeking to devour, but the church has stopped resisting him, fighting him, and warning the sheep of God's pasture of the danger he poses. What do you think will happen? How do you see this playing out?

At least real sheep – the ones that get sheered of their wool – are smart enough to sense the wolf coming. They can smell him on the wind and they start to bleat. If you follow this train of thought to its rightful conclusion, many supposed Christians are dumber than real sheep, because not only don't they sense the enemy among them, they take the viper to their bosom and attempt to rehabilitate it, and understand it.

The devil doesn't want to be converted. Demons not only believe in God, they tremble at the thought of Him and their impending judgment. The knowledge of finality, the knowledge he will be judged and cast into the lake of fire only fuels the devil's hatred of you and me, and knowing that his time is running out, knowing that he's on the clock makes him a tireless, motivated adversary.

If the devil were not such a real and present danger, if he were not a threat to the very existence of the children of God, then there is a good chunk of the Bible that is pointless, and was merely included as filler, or to confuse believers.

We must take the Word at face value, and believe what it says over what our denominational edicts say, or what our pastors and evangelists teach. If you have to twist the Word to make it fit your ideology, then may I submit that your ideology is flawed. If you have to ignore entire swaths of Scripture in order to maintain the solidity of your argument, then may I submit that your argument is illusory and not tethered in truth.

The devil is not dormant, the devil is not on vacation, the devil is not distracted with managerial issues, the devil is actively attempting to dismantle the household of faith, and destroy every single child of God that he finds without their armor, or outside the purview of God's protection.

Is the devil attacking you relentlessly? Is the enemy making war against you at every turn? If it is so, then good! It is a good thing when the enemy attacks you because he sees you pose a danger to him. It is a good thing when the enemy resists you because fear makes him go on the offensive, and strike blindly.

If it makes you feel any better, or if there is any comfort to be had, know that you are not alone. There are many believers the world over who are engaged in the selfsame battle you are engaged in. There are many believers the world over who are constantly at war with the devil because just as any true predator would, he knows he is in danger of losing his foothold.

Contrary to the image he tries to portray, the devil is a defeated foe and he knows it. Although his agents, acolytes, and minions try to project an air of invincibility and superiority, the reality of their existence is dark, and grim and hollow. Theirs is a life absent peace and joy, a life lived for momentary, fleeting pleasures that do nothing in the way of building an amalgam of experiences worth looking back on with fulfillment.

The devil can only offer illusion. The devil can only offer momentary pleasure, but in a world that's all about the moment, all about the now, all about fulfilling its wants and desires, what the devil offers is appealing.

It ought not to be so with the children of God, yet far too often we see believers being seduced away by the things of this present world as though somewhere along the way they forgot about their temporal nature.

Tragic as it may be to acknowledge, the enemy knows the promises of God as well as if not better than most Christians. He knows his time is limited, and the closer we get to the end of all things the more rabid he will become against the saints.

> Romans 16:20, "And the God of peace will crush Satan under your feet shortly. The grace of our Lord Jesus Christ be with you. Amen."

If anything, this is the truth that haunts the devil. He realizes the finality of God's promise to His children in that He will crush Satan under our feet shortly, but until that time, it is incumbent upon us to be relentless in defending the truth of the gospel, to be sober, and to be vigilant. It is incumbent upon us to resist the devil, because we are not resisting him in vain. Once more we turn to the promise of God's word, and take strength from it.

> James 4:7, "Therefore submit to God. Resist the devil and he will flee from you."

There are two things we must do in order to make the devil flee from us as per the Word of God. The first of these is to submit to God. Sometimes things sound simpler than they truly are, and this is one of those times.

When the Word commands us to submit to God, the implication is that we must submit to God in all things. Submission in some areas of our lives is easier than in others, but in order to make the enemy flee from before you, your submission to God must be all- encompassing. God is not looking for partial submission. He desires total submission. Comprehensive submission to God includes absolutely everything, from your physical self, to your spiritual self, to your wants, desires, opinions, aspirations, dreams, and goals.

Everything must be in submission to God, for only then can God lead you where He desires you to go, and only then will you go without hesitation or complaint. When God gives a command it is to be obeyed without delay, and far too often in the time it takes us to second guess God, to question His intent, to try and circumvent what He commanded us to do in the first place, we lose our window of opportunity to fulfill our task.

Submit to God in all things, in the present, without equivocation, and you will know Him and feel Him on a more intimate level than ever before.

The second thing we must do in order to cause the devil to flee from before us is to resist him. James echoes Peter in this regard, and even Paul makes mention of the need to resist the devil and not give in to his devices.

In order to resist the devil, we must be aware of the way he operates, the way he attacks, and the means he uses to attempt the destruction of the household of faith.

By far, the single most employed tactic by the enemy and his minions against the household of faith, is that of counterfeit spirituality, false doctrine, false apostles, and false teaching. The reason it is used so often is because it works so well.

When much of the church would pay more attention to whether a purse is counterfeit than whether a doctrine is counterfeit it's no wonder so many embrace deception as truth, and darkness as light.

The devil lies, and he lies well. He teaches his acolytes to do likewise, mixing half-truth with outright deception, because he knows that if an unsuspecting believer bites, the hook is set, and he can drag them further and further away from the truth.

Of all the Apostles, Paul had to contend with deception within the household of faith the most. From his epistles to the Corinthians, to his epistle to the Romans, to his epistles to the Thessalonians, the Galatians, the Philippians, and the Colossians, Paul had to contend with some sort of deception attempting to worm its way into the fellowships he had established, nurtured, taught, and discipled.

> *2 Corinthians 11:13-15, "For such are false apostles, deceitful workers, transforming themselves into apostles of Christ. And no wonder! For Satan himself transforms himself in to an angel of light. Therefore it is no great thing if his ministers also transform themselves into ministers of righteousness whose end will be according to their works."*

It is because of these verses and many like it within the pages of Scripture that I do not buy into the whole well-meaning-but-deceived excuse when it comes to some of today's preachers and evangelists. If you do not preach the truth, you are not well meaning, you are not innocuous, and you are not harmless to the body of Christ.

If you preach heresy you are a heretic. If you preach deception you are a deceiver. If you preach something contrary to the Gospel of Christ, you are a false apostle whose end will be according to your work.

We cannot mince words or play games with such serious matters. We cannot excuse outright deception within the house of God because we don't want to rock the boat or because the individual spouting said heresy is beloved by a certain denomination.

> *Philippians 3:18-19, "For many walk, of whom I have told you often, and now tell you even weeping; that they are the enemies of the cross of Christ: whose end is*

destruction, whose god is their belly, and whose glory is in their shame – who set their mind on earthly things."

Make that sound inoffensive! Make that sound harmless! You can't really twist *'enemies of the cross of Christ'* to mean something neutral or good no matter how much you spin it.

When we give leeway to deceivers they will only continue to deceive. When we abstain from voicing dissent upon hearing outright heresy spewed from behind pulpits, we are enabling them, strengthening their hand, and allowing them to go about the Satan's work.

Just from this passage in Philippians alone you can disqualify ninety percent the current televangelist crop, and rightly identify them as enemies of the cross of Christ.

Within the span of two verses Paul not only warns of deceivers, and that they abound, but he tells us what to look for in order to identify them as such.

If a preacher's god is his belly, if all he talks about is possessions and positions, if all he talks about is bigger homes and finer cars, if all he talks about is diamond rings and leer jets, if all he does is find new ways to fleece the sheep and ask them for money, then he is an enemy of the cross of Christ, by Paul's definition.

If a preacher glories in his shame, meaning he not only justifies his sinfulness, he plays it down and continues to minister as though he had not transgressed, brushing it off as though he had not trampled the Son of God underfoot, he is an enemy of the cross of Christ, by Paul's definition.

If a preacher has set his mind on earthly things perpetually focusing on this present life, on ways and means by which you can make the flesh feel at ease, and constructs ways by which you can live as the world but somehow still belong to God, he is an enemy of the cross of Christ, by Paul's definition.

We cannot circumvent the written Word because we don't like what it says, or because it shines the light of truth on one of our preferred evangelists or pastors. We cannot pretend as though these verses are not in the Bible simply because it will mean having to confront the lie, and stand up for the truth of Christ.

Another way by which Satan and his acolytes disrupt the household of faith and attempt to disillusion believers is by sowing doubt among the ranks. It worked well enough with Eve, and the devil is smart enough to know that if it's not broke you shouldn't try to fix it.

Doubt is a powerful tool in the enemy's arsenal because if he can plant the seed of doubt in someone's heart that seed will germinate and grow and yield fruit.

The devil attempts to sow a myriad of doubts into the hearts and minds of believers on a daily basis. From doubt as to whether or not God loves them, to doubt as to whether or not they are saved, to doubt as to whether or not God is with them through their current struggle, the end result of all unchecked doubt is the same.

Doubt causes a rift in the trust that we've established with God, and rather than know that He is there to catch us if we fall, He is there to comfort us if we ache, we begin to question whether or not this is really the case.

I've counseled enough married couples throughout my life to know that the root cause of most marital strife is the seed of doubt. When doubt rears its ugly head the individual is compelled to look for signs and patterns to validate their doubt, and even when none exist they try to make them up out of thin air because the need for validation of one's emotions is a powerful one.

As such, even if the husband or the wife are as faithful as ever, because a seed of doubt as to their faithfulness has crept in, they start to look for signs, for patterns, for something they can grasp at and build upon to the point that it explodes into a shouting match and accusations of infidelity.

The reason I mention this is because doubt regarding spiritual things works very similarly to doubt regarding the physical, and the antidote for doubt is likewise similar in both the physical and spiritual.

The first way by which we kill off the seed of doubt before it has a chance to take root is to know the character and nature of either the individual in question, or of God Himself if the matter is a spiritual one.

Knowledge of God not only breeds and encourages trust, it cements it to the point that it become unshakeable. I know my God well enough to know that He will see me through the storm because he has done it consistently throughout my life. I know that my Redeemer lives because I fellowship and commune with Him not sporadically or once in a while, but every single day without exception.

Whenever the enemy comes in like a flood attempting to sow doubt in your heart learn to identify him, understand the action for what it is, then meditate upon the God you know, the God of the Bible, the unchanging, ever faithful, ever true God who has never failed you. Having done that, resist the devil, rebuke him, and he will flee, having seen his plan be brought to naught.

As believers we sometimes forget that Satan transforms himself into an angel of light, and so we expect the in-your-face I'm-the-devil-and-here-are-my-horns sort of attack, when the enemy's attacks are more subtle, playing on our weaknesses and our ignorance of God and who he truly is.

If Satan presented himself as he truly was and did not employ guile and deception, how many people do you think would be seduced away from the truth?

It seems the enemy knows what many believers fail to grasp when it comes to deception. Deception need not be blatant from the get go. One need only deviate an inch off the path, and given enough time they will have found themselves in the desert, far removed from any semblance of God.

It begins with the knowing and willful compromise of a single truth, then it simply snowballs from there.

Our adversary is patient and cunning. Just like the lion to which he is compared in Scripture he stalks his prey and waits for just the right moment to pounce, and come in for the kill.

The enemy will never attack you when you are at your strongest because like any coward is likely to do he senses weakness and preys upon it. It is at your lowest, at your weakest, when you are most distracted and disengaged that the enemy will throw everything he has your way hoping to cause you to stumble, and once he has you down he will do everything he can to keep you there.

Once we understand who the enemy is, what his intent is, and the weapons he employs against the children of God, not only are we able to see him coming from a mile away, we strip him of the element of surprise, and the possibility of coming in close and doing the most harm.

There are certain Bible passages that are yet to be fulfilled that should give us all reason for pause and ignite in us an overwhelming desire to prepare against the coming onslaught of the enemy. We have yet to see the worst the devil has to throw at us, and this is a reality with which we must contend.

If we are wise, the knowledge of this truth will spur us to an ever increasing state of readiness and vigilance. If we are unwise, we will simply lay all our hopes in the baseless fable of being caught away before the Word says we will.

Although the following may be the topic for an entirely different book, contextually speaking it must be mentioned just so I know I have no blood on my hands, or make myself guilty of the sin of omission.

The church isn't going anywhere any time soon, and nowhere in scripture is it implied that we will somehow be able to circumvent the final battle.

John 17:15, "I do not pray that you should take them out of the world, but that You should keep them from the evil one."

2 Thessalonians 2:1-4, "Now, brethren, concerning the coming of our Lord Jesus Christ and our gathering together to Him, we ask you, not to be soon shaken in mind or troubled, either by spirit or by word or by letter, as if from us, as though the day of Christ had come. Let no one deceive you by any means; for that Day will not come unless the falling away comes first and the man of sin is revealed, the son of perdition, who opposes and exalts himself above all that is called God or that is worshipped, so that he sits as God in the temple of God showing himself that he is God."

But we couldn't live with the simplicity of the Gospel, could we? We couldn't just believe the Word of God when it said that the day would not come unless the falling away came first, and the man of sin was revealed. We had to concoct fables and invent signs, and look to the stars and the moons until we got night blindness just so we could believe it when we told others that they will be spirited away before any of these troublesome bits.

We couldn't tell the church to prepare for battle, to steel itself and stand, because that would be unloving and unkind to do. We couldn't tell the church that soon it would cost them everything to call themselves a son or daughter of the Most High God because for the past quarter century we've beaten the drum of prosperity until all we could equate Jesus with was prosperity and excess, and nothing deeper than that.

We manufactured a shallow spirituality and passed it off as the true Gospel thinking we were doing God a service by bringing more tithers into our halls of desecration while all the while we were doing the devil's bidding, having become enemies of the cross of Christ in word and in deed.

The new breed of 'Christian' wants nothing of righteousness, or sanctification, or holiness. They want to be entertained, they want to be made to feel good, and they want to be validated in their sin so they will never have to abandon the things of this world for the things of God.

I don't know about you but that looks a lot like a great falling away to me.

Many are awaiting an abandoning of the churches, an emptying out of congregations before they can definitively say it is a falling away, but there must be an abandoning of truth first before there can be an abandoning of congregations, and I fear the abandoning of truth has been upon us for many a year now.

We will see the Godless temples of hedonism we have erected for our own glory empty out soon enough, because once men depart from truth there is nothing to keep them in a supposed house of God.

Know the enemy for yourself. Don't wait for someone else to point him out, and don't wait for someone else to warn you of his impending attacks. It is your duty to be vigilant, it is your duty to be sober, it is your duty to be alert enough to see the enemy coming long before he is within striking distance.

Spiritual surrogacy doesn't work. Counting on others to be your eyes and ears in battle doesn't work. It is incumbent upon you as an individual to know how to spot the enemy and his minions and turn away from them.

Once you know what to look for it's not difficult to tell who is of the light and who is of the dark. Once you know what to look for it's not difficult to tell who is speaking truth and who is promoting heresy.

We know what to look for by diligently studying the word of God and understanding the symptomology of the enemies of the cross of Christ. There are always telltale signs, there are always patterns that become apparent over time, because the devil cannot hide his intent forever.

> *2 Timothy 3:1-7, "But know this, that in the last days perilous times will come: for men will be lovers of themselves, lovers of money, boasters, proud, blasphemers, disobedient to parents, unthankful, unholy, unloving, unforgiving, slanderers, without self-control, brutal, despisers of good, traitors, headstrong, haughty, lovers of pleasure rather than lovers of God, having a form of godliness but denying its power. And from such people turn away! For of this sort are those who creep into households and make captives of gullible women loaded down with sins, led away by various lusts, always learning and never able to come to the knowledge of the truth."*

> *2 Timothy 4:3-4, "For the time will come when they will not endure sound doctrine, but according to their own desires, because they have itching ears, they will heap up*

for themselves teachers; and they will turn their ears away from the truth, and be turned aside to fables."

If you had any doubt as to what you should be looking to avoid, this handful of verses in Paul's second letter to Timothy sums it up quite nicely. What many believers fail to realize is that when Paul was writing about the last days he was doing so prophetically, and when he spoke of men who would be lovers of self, lovers of money, boasters, proud, blasphemers, and the rest of the dark list of sins, he was writing about these things being present within the church, not without the church.

Lovers of money existed in the world even in Paul's day, as did lovers of self, as did traitors and lovers of pleasure rather than lovers of God, but the paramount difference between that time and the last days is that these things would be occurring within the church itself.

One need only to give a passing glance to the current spiritual condition of the church to realize that Paul's prophecy has come to pass, and is continuing to come to pass before our very eyes. All the things he warned of are currently taking places among men and women who name the name of Christ and self-identify as Christians.

As those who know not to defile themselves with the things of this world, as those who know not to court or flirt with sin, we are commanded to turn away from such individuals and have nothing to do with them.

The reason for this is that compromise is oftentimes communicable. If one soldier stands fast on the ramparts while thirty others are sleeping, eventually the watchful soldier will begin to wonder to himself what the harm would be if he too took a nap, if he too got off his feet for a little while, if he too took of his armor and allowed himself to relax.

Those of whom Paul writes, those who creep into households and who are never able to come to the knowledge of the truth, are not doing what they do out of ignorance, or with good intentions. It is not our duty to try and reason with them, or make them see the error of their ways. Our duty is to turn away from them, God's duty is to judge them righteously for causing little ones to stumble.

The Word does not command us to be loving toward the darkness, nor does it command us to be loving toward sin. We are not commanded to embrace the devil while holding our noses; we are commanded to live sanctified, holy lives as unto Him and let nothing deter us from this single-minded pursuit.

CHAPTER ELEVEN

DO YOU KNOW YOUR OBJECTIVE?

Every soldier who has ever stepped onto the battlefield had a very clear mission objective. He knew what his duty entailed, what his goal was, what he wanted to accomplish by being there, and it was not some vague, amorphous thing that changed with the current. It was a certainty about which there was no ambiguity. Every man who has ever fought in battle has fought to obtain victory. No one ever steps onto the battlefield intent on losing, yet one side always loses. This is a sobering reality and one we cannot overlook, or consider lightly.

In every battle there is a winner and a loser; there are those who are conquered, and there are those who conquer. In battle you don't get a participation trophy. There are no *also ran* ribbons handed out to those who lost after the war, and there is no do over.

The spiritual battle you and I are now entangled in must become as real to us, as would an actual, physical war on our own soil. It's one thing to hear of war ten thousand miles away, on a different continent, fought by men who you will never know, it's another when the war is brought home, when it's in one's city, and neighborhoods, and streets.

If we rightly discern between eternity and this present, temporal existence, we would even conclude that the stakes are astronomically higher in the spiritual than they are in the physical. This present life has an expiration date. We know it from the moment we are old enough to perceive anything of the world around us, and from the instant our parents dress us in itchy, drab, clothing and bring us along to a family member's funeral.

Eternity, on the other hand, is forever. Forever is a long time, and seeing as the alternative to heaven is the outer darkness where there is gnashing of teeth, the worm never dies, and the fire is not quenched, I would presume to conclude that we should do our utmost to be welcomed into the former rather than cast into the latter.

I realize the devil's public relations department has been working overtime trying to make hell sound appealing, but from what we read in the Word it doesn't much sound like the party palace the agents of darkness insist it's going to be, does it?

The prize for which we fight is commensurate with the size and scope of the battle itself. We do not wage the war we wage for trinkets and baubles. We do not forfeit this present life, deny our aspirations and dreams, suffer persecution, endure hardships, become outcasts of society and live marginalized lives for having stood on the foundation of Christ, just to get a paper hat and some confetti at the end of it all.

We know what we are fighting for. We know what we are living for, and we know what we are willing to die for. The prize that awaits each of us at the end of our race, the crown that awaits each of us at the end of our struggle is not some paltry thing we will look upon with dissatisfaction and disappointment.

We wage war against the darkness, we stand firm against the tide of the enemy, we attack, we pull down strongholds, we disrupt the plans of the evil one because it is our duty, it is our mission, it is our objective, and we know that He who has sent us into battle, He who leads the charge against Satan is neither stingy nor miserly when it comes to rewarding each one according to their work.

Now that you have learned what it is to fight, determined how far you are willing to go, have mastered your weapons, have realized your authority, have built up your endurance, have learned the value of knowing oneself, have intimately come to know who your general is as well as who your enemy is, the one question that remains is whether or not you know what your objective is.

What is the mission? What is it that we are commanded and expected to do for the kingdom of God? In every skirmish, in every war, there is an overarching objective. There is always something that is expected of every soldier standing on the battlefield. There are also those who get assigned special missions, unique tasks, but those missions and tasks are always in service of the overarching objective and never work against it.

The pursuit and achieving of the objective must be paramount in every command you are given, every task you are tasked with, and every order you receive. If any of what you are you are commanded to do conflicts with the overarching objective, know that somehow, somewhere the enemy has infiltrated the command structure and is giving false orders.

God will not tell you to do something contrary to His Word or contrary to His nature. God will not command you to undertake a mission that goes against what has already been established as the mission objective for His entire army.

On occasion I meet individuals who insist that God told them to abandon their families, their wives and their children, all so they could go preach the gospel on some beach somewhere, and nevermore consider the lives they ruined. This type of conversation never ends on a positive note, because in each case I would have been remiss if I did not point out that God would never ask you to abandon what He has blessed and sanctioned, what He takes joy and pleasure in, what He has granted you as one of the greatest gifts that can be bestowed upon an individual.

He gave you a son, He gave you a daughter, He gave you a loving wife, He gave you a family. What makes you think, even for one second, that God would ask you to abandon them so you could go to Hawaii and hand out Jack Chick tracts?

God is wise enough to send someone not obliged to provide and care for a family to do this task, and leave you to be the head of your household and a father to your children.

Again, and I reiterate this because it is important, God will never ask you to do something contrary to His nature. He will never ask you to perform a task that goes against His character.

That said, we return to the foremost question of this chapter, namely, do you know your mission objective? In order to rightly determine what our mission objective is, we must first acknowledge certain truths.

The first truth we must acknowledge is that we are in enemy territory. This is not a battle on our own turf, it is a battle on the enemy's turf, and he knows the layout of his terrain better than you ever will. He knows where the booby traps are placed, he knows where the terrain becomes uneven, he knows where the snares are, he knows the best points of attack, and he uses all these against the army of God on a daily basis.

If it helps, think of your church fellowship as the green zone, the base camp, and the rest of the world as the warzone itself. You return to the green zone when you need to rearm, bandage wounds, have some fellowship with your fellow brothers in arms, but the battle is always beyond the walls of the green zone, beyond the walls of the church.

If today's modern church spent as much time fighting in the warzone as they do in the green zone, then perhaps the enemy would not be mocking the church at every turn, and taking precious ground from us with every encounter.

1 John 5:19, "We know that we are of God, and the whole world lies under the sway of the wicked one."

There is an us and there is a them. The Word of God is very explicit on this point, and there is no room to see it otherwise. We know that we are of God. This is who we are, this is where we belong, our identity is certain, and there is nothing anyone can say or do to change it. We don't hope that we are of God, we don't assume that we are of God, we don't question whether we are of God, we know that we are of God.

Just as we know that we are of God, we likewise know that the whole world lies under the sway of the wicked one. There is no third party system, there is no neutral territory wherein some don't know that they are of God but aren't under the sway of the wicked one. You're either of God, or you are not.

You either stand against the darkness or you are darkness.

One of our first mission objectives is to stand. Simple as it may sound, those who know how to stand their ground and stare down the whirlwind are few and far in between. When we are commanded to stand, we are not told to stand only when there is no enemy present, or when victory is assured, or when standing takes no effort on our part. We are told to stand, and do our utmost to remain standing even in the maelstrom, even in the battle, even when all you can see is flashes of swords, and all you can hear is the whizzing of arrows.

It takes courage to stand your ground. It takes boldness to say to the devil himself that he will not steal from you what God has entrusted you to protect and keep. Does this mean you will never again be fearful in the midst of battle? No, but what it does mean is that by the grace and power of God you will overcome your fear, you will conquer it, and you will do your duty regardless of your emotions.

Whatever it is you are defending need not have value in and of itself, it has value because God gave it to you, and entrusted you to defend it. We're not talking about defending a cargo ship full of gold, but even something as seemingly irrelevant as a piece of ground full of lentils.

Among David's mighty men there was one named Eleazar the son of Dodo the Ahohite. If not for his act of valor, Eleazar might never have been remembered, his name long forgotten even by his own kin. But during the protracted war with the Philistines Eleazar did something remarkable on behalf of something that at first glance didn't seem worth risking one's life for.

> 1 Chronicles 11:12-14, "After him was Eleazar the son of Dodo, the Ahohite, who was one of the three mighty men. He was with David at Pasdammim. Now there the Philistines were gathered for battle, and there was a piece of ground full of barley. And the people fled from the Philistines. But they stationed themselves in the midst of that field, defended it, and killed the Philistines. And the Lord saved them by a great deliverance."

For anyone not understanding the notion of duty this passage might be difficult to come to terms with. These men did not choose to make their stand defending a city, these men did not choose to make their stand defending Jerusalem, they chose to make their stand defending a piece of ground full of barley.

All the other people had fled from the Philistines, the Philistines had gathered for battle, yet here these men were, stationing themselves in the midst of a barley field ready to defend it to the death.

For those who were not soldiers, for those who were not warriors, it was just easier to let the Philistines have the piece of ground than try to defend it. For those who did not know what it was to fight, the implied cost of defending a handful of barley was just too high, and so they chose to flee and give up their territory.

To David and Eleazar, however, it was not about the barley. It wasn't even about the piece of ground. It was about the principle of giving up ground, any ground, to the enemy. These men had purposed in their hearts that they would give absolutely nothing to the enemy, they would surrender nothing to the Philistines, and they were willing to pay the ultimate price in order to make certain of it.

There is a profound spiritual principle in what David and Eleazar did that applies to our mission objective and what our attitude ought to be regarding giving up anything to the enemy. No matter what, no matter how small, no matter how seemingly insignificant, we leave nothing for the devil, and we surrender nothing to him.

Don't do the devil any favors because he is certain not to do you any. Be willing to make your stand and fight the darkness even over something others might consider small and ultimately irrelevant, because the enemy will know that if he wants anything from you be it great or be it small, he'll have to fight you for it.

For as far back as I can remember, at least in my lifetime the church has been on the retreat, giving up territory after territory because someone somewhere decided it was too small a thing to start a fight over, it was too small a thing to make a stand about.

We surrendered first one thing, then another, each subsequently bigger than the last, all the while soothing our cowardice with the notion that one of these days we would make our stand, one of these days we would decide that enough was enough, one of these days we'd show that wily devil we mean business.

Tragically, as yet, that day has not come, and with each passing season we retreat ever more, giving up more territory to the devil because we realized it was just easier to run away than to stand one's ground. We decided that discretion was the better part of valor, somehow ignoring the fact that this is the coward's credo, and there is no room in God's army for cowards.

We refused to defend the small things because we thought them unworthy of our efforts, and the more ground we gave up the bolder the enemy became. Now the enemy is even threatening to breach the walls and overrun the household of faith itself, and still nothing from large swaths of supposed believers.

One of your first mission objectives as you find yourself behind enemy lines is to defend truth, and stand your ground whenever you encounter the enemy and his minions.

I realize the notion of speaking up and taking a stand for what is true and righteous and pure is outside the comfort zone of some individuals, and truth be known I don't much like confrontation either, but some things must be done whether we're comfortable doing them or not, and being bold for the cause of Christ is one of those things.

Our duty isn't to do the easy thing, the comfortable thing, or the popular thing. Our duty as soldiers of Jesus is to do the right thing.

No one had to tell David and Eleazar what the right thing was. They didn't have to wait for a message from the Lord, they didn't need to get confirmation, they didn't need to feel good about it. They knew what the right thing to do was, and they did it uncertain of the outcome of their endeavor.

The only thing they knew they had to do, because it was the right thing to do, was to defend the piece of ground full of barely.

No one assured of any victory, no one assured them of success, they simply did their part, and in doing the right and noble thing the Lord saved them by a great deliverance.

The world as we know it is coming apart at the seams. Everywhere you look it seems as though there is a powder keg just waiting for a lit match. In the ensuing chaos the Children of God must stand out as lights in the darkness. They must be the ones to speak truth in a sea of lies, and to be the salt the earth so desperately needs.

Our secondary mission objective as soldiers of Christ, is to bring glory to our General in every area of our lives. It is because we are His soldiers that we are called upon to conduct ourselves in an upright and holy manner. It is because we are His soldiers that He demands we be sanctified and set apart. It is because we are His soldiers that His expectations regarding us are higher than for anyone else. His standard is high and He demands excellence because we represent Him in this dying world.

There is a code of conduct for the believer, just as there is a code of conduct for those who join any branch of the military today. This code of conduct is in place so men might know what is acceptable as one wearing the uniform, and what is not acceptable and punishable in a military tribunal.

Philippians 1:27-28, "Only let your conduct be worthy of the gospel of Christ, so that whether I come and see you or am absent, I may hear of your affairs, that you stand fast in one spirit, with one mind, striving together for the faith of the gospel, and not in any way terrified by your adversaries, which is to them a proof of perdition, but to you of salvation, and that from God."

If we were to go to the Greek translation of this passage we would discover that when Paul says those at Philippi ought to have a conduct worthy of the gospel of Christ, it literally meant that they ought to behave as citizens.

If you want to read this passage a different way, one that is contextually significant insofar as our discussion regarding bringing glory to God is concerned, Paul is telling those at Philippi to behave as citizens in a manner worthy of the gospel of Christ.

If you are of Christ, don't live like the world. If you are of Christ, don't act like the world. If you are of Christ, don't speak like the world. You are a citizen of the Kingdom of God, behave like it, act like it, speak like it. Whether in the presence of other believers or by yourself, whether surrounded by heathens or those of mixed faiths your duty is still to behave as a citizen of heaven worthy of the gospel of Christ.

Historical records show that Philippi was a Roman colony and as was the case with most colonies of the time, the citizenry was likely either retired soldiers from the Roman legions, or transplanted Romans. Even though they were far from Rome, even though they were not likely to ever see Rome again, because they were citizens of Rome they were expected to behave as citizens of Rome throughout.

We are a colony of light in a sea of darkness. As believers we are not citizens of any one nation, we are citizens of heaven. God has every right to expect us to behave as citizens of heaven during the time of our sojourning here, because all we do reflects on Him.

When men forget this truth they begin to behave as the heathen, and sooner or later it is the heathen who will point out the fact that having claimed a heavenly citizenship you ought to be markedly different from them. Few things are more shameful for a citizen of heaven than to be called out by a godless individual for their conduct and actions.

We've lost sight of what it means to be sanctified, or perhaps we're just willfully ignoring its definition because we like the ways of the heathen too much to surrender them altogether and live as God would have us live.

1 Peter 1:17-19, "And if you call on the Father, who without partiality judges according to each one's work, conduct yourselves throughout the time of your sojourning here in fear; knowing that you were not redeemed with corruptible things, like silver or gold, from your aimless conduct received by tradition from your fathers, but with the precious blood of Christ, as of a lamb without blemish and without spot."

A price was paid that you might call yourself a son of God. A price was paid that you might call yourself a daughter of God. Be aware and cognizant of the price that was paid, for it was not something corruptible like silver or gold. The price that was paid so that you and I might have the honor of being citizens of heaven was the blood of Christ the Son of God, He who was without spot or blemish.

Pseudo-intellectuals can throw Christian liberty in my face all they want for the sinfulness in which they choose to participate, but just because you may have the liberty to do something doesn't mean you should do it.

Consider the price that was paid and who paid it before you decide to bring shame to the household of faith. Consider the price that was paid and who paid it before you decide to besmirch the name and character of God Himself by your selfish actions, knowing that men throughout will associate you with Him because of your previous proclamations.

How much of a sway must sin have over an individual for them not to take into account that they are conducting themselves in an unworthy manner, and that their actions are in direct opposition to how the Word of God says we ought to live?

Being men and women of character, being men of women who pursue righteousness, being men and women who desire sanctification, are not things only the excessively devout are to do, they are the least any of us who name the name of Christ are commanded to do.

We are Ambassadors of Christ on this earth. We represent Jesus, and are sanctioned to do so by Him, and those among whom we represent Him know this truth from the outright.

Is your life bringing glory to God? Is your conduct bringing glory to God? Are your associations, the places you frequent, your hobbies, how you spend your leisure time, what you invest your disposable income in, are all these bringing glory to God? If not, then why not?

What of this earth has wormed its way into your heart that you bring no glory to God in a certain segment of your life? What of this earth has wormed its way into your heart that in a given area men look at you and do not see Jesus in you?

If you've put on the uniform, don't sully it. If you represent Christ on this earth than do your utmost to make certain that your conduct is worthy of His name and His sacrifice.

Our final mission objective is to endure to the end. Desertion is not an option, nor is bowing out of the battle. We cannot fake an injury, or fail a mental competency test, or run to Canada to avoid the draft for that matter.

Once we are entangled in this fiercest of wars we have no choice but to see it through to its conclusion. Anything less, and we become prey, victims of the enemy's many slings and arrows, just another statistic added to the body count of believers who thought they had the option of being observers, conscientious or otherwise.

To the enemy, your being unarmed just makes you an easier target. It does nothing in the way of preventing him from felling you where you stand, because the enemy does not follow the Geneva convention, or any other wartime rules and regulations men's armies adhere to.

The importance of enduring to the end, even unto death, cannot be overemphasized, because the Word is clear that he who endures to the end will be saved, he who endures to the end will receive a crown of victory.

James 1:12, "Blessed is the man who endures temptation; for when he has been proved, he will receive the crown of life which the Lord has promised to those who love Him."

Revelation 2:10, "Do not fear any of those things which you are about to suffer. Indeed, the devil is about to throw some of you into prison, that you may be tested, and you will have tribulation ten days. Be faithful until death, and I will give you the crown of life."

"But how can we not be afraid? How can we not be troubled by the thought that some of us will get thrown into prison, and some of us will even have to endure to the death?"

Because through it all God is with us. Because our General, our heavenly Father, the Great I Am will never leave our side, He will never abandon us, and it is He who will give us the strength to persevere and overcome.

Isaiah 43:2-3, "When you pass through the waters, I will be with you; and through the rivers, they shall not overflow you. When you walk through the fire, you shall not be burned, nor shall the flame scorch you. For I am the Lord your God, the Holy One of Israel, your Savior."

Psalm 91:9-11, "Because you have made the Lord, who is my refuge, even the Most High, your habitation, no evil shall befall you, nor shall any plague come near your dwelling; for He shall give His angels charge over you, to keep you in all your ways."